Looking Sideways at God

Frank Pagden is a Methodist minister who works as a presenter and producer for BBC Radio Leeds where he is responsible for religious and other broadcasting. As a result he is well known as a broadcaster, preacher and speaker in Yorkshire. He is one of the pioneers of religious local radio, having started with Radio Leeds in 1968. He also edits the Christian Comment page on BBC Ceefax. *Looking Sideways at God* is his first book.

Looking Sideways at GOD

Frank Pagden

First published 1985
Triangle/SPCK
Holy Trinity Church
London NW1 4DU

British Library Cataloguing in Publication Data

Pagden, Frank
Looking sideways at God.
1. Theology, Doctrinal
I. Title
230 BT77.3

ISBN 0-281-04198-7

Typeset by Photobooks (Bristol) Ltd, Bristol
Printed in Great Britain by
Hazell, Watson & Viney Limited
Member of the BPCC Group
Aylesbury, Bucks

To my best friends, my wife and children

Contents

Introduction

When I was at school a master once pinned me to the wall with a gimlet look and said, 'If there's two ways of doing a thing, you'll be guaranteed to find the third!' It was a charge I couldn't deny, for somehow, by guess and by God, I usually ended up with the right answer, but hardly ever got to it in the proper way. As those were the days when marks tended to be awarded for method rather than conclusions, it didn't bode well for my scholastic career.

This continued at college when the lecturers would return my essays with remarks like, 'You sit too lightly on this authority, or that.' One glimmer of light was a tutor, now an eminent church leader, who happily marked my Greek translation of 'Who was that lady I saw you with last night . . .?' and returned the compliment by finding an incredible seventeen mistakes in it.

Ever since, read and study as I will, it has not been the solid body of knowledge itself which has fascinated me, but rather the grain on its surface, and the flowers growing in the cracks. I weakly defend this by comparing it to an expert gardener who can judge the condition of the soil by the weeds growing on it, without disturbing the soil. In theology one can find insights on the surface which can be buried when one starts solid shovelling.

This has naturally influenced how my understanding of God has developed. It is not original thought – God had the only original thought, and we are it – but rather a look at the Christian faith through half-closed eyes with my head on one side.

I am, of course, hugely in the debt of the speakers at whose feet I have sat, the people I have met, and the books I have read. A particular influence has been Professor D.M. Baillie's book *God was in Christ*.

English people are supposed to love paradoxes and amiable eccentrics, so perhaps I am not the only one who takes a delight in the unexpected view, is amused by the incongruous, and finds inspiration by looking at God sideways.

F.P.

1 *Unscrewing the Inscrutable*

'Mum,' said the little girl, 'was God married and did he have a daddy?' and so the little child puts her finger on the puzzle that has baffled grown up minds since the world began.

We live in a world of cause and effect. Scientists search for the causes of the effects that they see, for they know that there must be a cause; that is how the world is made. When they find it, they then discover that the cause they have isolated is itself the effect of another cause further back still.

My toe hurts. Why? Because I'm playing cricket and I have dropped my bat on it. Why did I drop the bat? Because I have not got the close combination of a quick eye and muscular co-ordination to be admired in good cricketers. Why haven't I got it? Because of the way I'm made. Why am I made this way? Because of heredity. But why are my genes different from other people's, and how did mine separate from theirs?

And so it goes on, until eventually we reach the primal beginning, and when we get there we discover a mystery – a cause that was not caused by something else. Some say that everything began with a 'big bang'. If we accept that for the moment, we are forced to ask, 'Who lit the fuse?' I once had a most enjoyable argument in an army barrack room with the squad atheist. 'Atoms are only whizzing electrical charges, thought is just minute charges between brain cells, so this world is just one enormous thought,' he said with the glint of the perfect argument in his eye. 'OK,' I replied. 'Who thunk it?'

So, rephrase it as we like, we are still face to face with

something completely beyond our experience; an 'uncaused' first cause. It is a contradiction in terms, a paradox. There must be an answer somewhere, but it cannot be a logical answer because our logic, and therefore our language, has reached a dead stop.

So let us start another line of thought. If we look up at the stars on a clear night we can see thousands of what we are told are vast suns, and with a pair of binoculars thousands or millions more become visible, seeming to go on for ever. This raises the question, 'Does space finish? Is there a place way out there where space stops?' Our logical minds tell us that it must stop somewhere because we cannot imagine the infinity of it going on forever. Yet if space does end somewhere, what is outside it?

There is a theory that space is curved, and that the smallest stars that can be seen are really (and the cynics love this) our own backsides! But this doesn't answer the question either, for even if space is circular, what is outside the circle? So again we hit the boundary of logic – a paradox.

Think of time. Will it ever come to an end? Will there ever come a moment when all clocks stop and time itself ceases to exist? Our human minds tell us that it is inconceivable that it should go on for ever, yet if it stops – what happens afterwards? Yet again the human mind seizes up.

We have to conclude that if we think in a straight line in any direction we shall in the end reach the limits of our intellect and confront a paradox. We live on an island of logic surrounded by a sea of paradox.

There once was an American huckster who was introduced as 'Professor Hemplestein who knows the unknowable, thinks the unthinkable and unscrews the inscrutable.' Is it possible for ordinary human beings to unscrew the inscrutable paradoxes of truth? The Christian answer, modestly put, must be 'Yes'. But we cannot do it with logic and language.

Those instruments can carry us only so far before they break down. It is like driving a car. You may drive a car in a (more or less) straight line in any direction for quite a way, but eventually you will reach the sea and you will be forced to stop. Your vehicle is unsuited and incapable of taking you further. If you want to go on, you must change vehicles and get into a boat.

This is what religion is all about, for it recognizes that the deepest, and therefore most real, questions are set in this background of mystery and paradox, and it is in this medium that we believe God lives.

Holy, profound, and militant people argued for centuries to define the nature of God. They eventually achieved the formula 'Three in One, and One in Three', which is logical nonsense. Even when expanded to that convoluted cat's cradle of jargon called the Athanasian Creed, which according to the Book of Common Prayer had to be repeated on festival days, it is still nonsense. When it says, 'He therefore that will be saved, must thus think of the Trinity', heaven help us all.

How much better to appreciate that God is a paradox and cannot be put into words.

The central core of Christianity, some say its central scandal, lies in the belief that Jesus was, and is, divine. If this is accepted, then we see at the cradle in Bethlehem a whole bundle of paradoxes. Here is the all-wise becoming ignorant, the most powerful becoming helpless, the God who made our home becoming homeless. As we think of Mary patting the baby's back to make him burp, we see the most dominant becoming the most vulnerable – here is a baby who is both human and divine, God and man, a clear, mind-boggling contradiction. Yet this is exactly how we would expect a God who lives in paradox to show himself.

Every Christian knows that our experience of God, however variable it may be from one person to another, has the mark of paradox upon it. For instance, God deals with us in such a way that we seem to be totally in control of our own decisions; we make up our own minds. Yet we can look back and see that God has led us step by step to where he wants us to be, at the time he wants us to be there. We know in our own lives the truth of the words from the Book of Common Prayer, 'His service is perfect freedom.'

It seems, and indeed it *is*, incredible that the God who, as James Wheldon Johnson put it, 'flung the ball of light against the darkness, spangling the night with the moon and stars', should be the same God who knows us so intimately that, in Jesus' words, 'even the hairs of your head are numbered'. To accept that God can do one or the other may be logical; but to believe both at the same time goes beyond logic and faces us again with a paradox.

If the first and greatest paradox is the existence of God, the second must be the mystery of pain and suffering. When we think of the greatest crimes against humanity - Stalin's purges, Hitler's holocaust, China, Cambodia - we wonder how many millions of those who died did so crying to God for help. Yet there was no answer. How can this be? Is God incompetent or unloving? There is no logical answer to this most horrifying of questions, either on this mass scale, or on the equally agonizing scale of someone suffering close to us. It is a paradox, a mystery to which human thought, however compassionate, can find no answer.

It is at this point that we must part company with some, at least, of the philosophers of this world. Christianity is not anti-logic, but will use logic as far as it goes, and then go beyond it. The Almighty gave us heads and expects us to use them properly, so there can be no excuse for muddled and lazy thinking, or false paradoxes being used to cover up inconvenient sense.

The difference lies in the philosopher's assumption that

logic is the only way to appreciate reality, and that if a thing is not logical it is nonsense, cannot exist and cannot be appreciated. I cannot understand Chinese, which is my cultural loss. To me, those pictograms are just pretty brush strokes, and do not convey any meaning at all. But even so, it would be highly arrogant of me to assume that because I, in my ignorance, don't understand Chinese, the language is therefore nonsense; and that because it is nonsense it doesn't exist as a form of communication.

No Christian should decry logic and sense. G.K. Chesterton described Father Brown unmasking Flambeau with the words, 'I knew you weren't a priest, because you attacked reason – it's bad theology.' Logic is God-given; it must be respected and used properly. Nevertheless, a Christian *does* attack the putting of reason on a pedestal and worshipping it. For reality is more than reason, God is greater than logic, and to stop at the boundaries of reason is to miss the broad sea of paradoxical truth. Perhaps this was in Jesus' mind when he praised God 'because you have hidden these things from the wise and learned and revealed them to little children'.

This is what religion is all about. The church – whether it has a spire and stands on the street corner, a name like 'Ebenezer' and is tucked down a side street, or is a borrowed room in a council flat – can only be religious if it is dealing with the mysteries of life: What is God? Who are we? What are we here for? What is our relationship with each other? Where are we going? These are religious questions that have no purely logical answers, for they are based on the logical unknown.

This doesn't mean, of course, that churches should spend all their time pondering the impossibilities; there is a proper and natural concern for social and community affairs. Christianity is not a religion with social aspects, it *is* a community religion. All its big words – Love, Reconciliation,

Father, Kingdom – emphasize this. Christians should always be active in righting injustices and helping the casualties. But even so, if they forget the central questions, and ignore the paradoxes, the church will find that it is no longer practising a religion and worshipping a God, but praising the human mind, and living an ethical code.

If, to return to the analogy of the car reaching the cliff, logic will no longer serve to get us closer to God, what will? If we have reached the shore of the infinity of truth, what new vehicle can we find to take us further? The answer is clear throughout the teaching of Jesus – faith. This is the boat which will let us launch out on the sea of paradox, and get us closer to the ultimate truth.

This is a beautiful answer to our problem, for faith does not depend on intelligence, education or influence. It is a quality that is available to old and young, clever and stupid – available, in fact, to all. The way Jesus put it, if anything it is biased in favour of the childlike, the innocent, the weak and the poor. Like the toddler who can open the 'child-proof' bottle that is beyond grandma, it is they, and those who have a childlike faith, who can unscrew the inscrutable and come nearest to our paradoxical God.

2 *Non-existent – but Easy*

Faith does not exist – not as an independent thing, that is. There are faithful people and faithless people; people who have faith in worthy things, and people who have faith in worthless things. Faith is an activity, a way of approaching things; not a quality that can be isolated and studied apart from people. It is a word that has no meaning except in human relationships.

Because it is used so much in religious circles, 'faith' may seem to be a religious word. But it isn't, for faith is a quality that we all use as the regular currency of our daily lives. We use it, for instance, every time we travel.

Electronic destination boards were installed at Euston station a little while ago. I was amused by a letter in a newspaper a few days afterwards. 'When I went for my train at Euston, the departure indicator said it was going to Rugby, the ticket collector and the notice on the platform said it was going to Coventry, the destination board on the train said Wolverhampton. I got off at Watford, went home and looked up the timetable to discover that it was actually going to Birmingham!'

Yet in spite of experiences of this kind, whenever we catch a train or wait at a bus stop we believe in what we see on the destination boards. Muddles and misinformation accepted, we have faith in what we see. We do so because we have no option. We cannot *prove* that the train is going to where we want, and indeed travel would be almost impossible if we tried. We use our faith whenever we travel because we have to in order to live our ordinary lives.

A recent tactic by irresponsible pressure groups is to tamper with containers on supermarket shelves, and poison the contents in order to blackmail the manufacturers. Naturally enough, this causes consternation among everyone, and this very shock wave illustrates the tremendous faith we have in the goods we buy in the shops. We pour our cereal into our breakfast bowls with gay abandon, and it never crosses our minds that there might be something wrong with it. We regard the food-tasters of medieval kings as long departed relics of a barbarous age. Yet, if we needed to *prove* that our food was healthy, we'd all have to employ one. But if we had to do that, we'd soon starve. So, as we must eat to live, we employ the quality of faith. We reason that, as this particular brand of cereal has been all right in the past, has got a good reputation, and is manufactured properly, we can justifiably believe that this particular portion in front of us is healthy – so we eat it.

In every facet of life we can show that faith is not something that we only use on Sundays. Everyone uses it every day. It is the grease which lubricates ordinary life and without it society would seize up solid.

When it comes to personal relationships, faith is more than a vital lubricant; it is a nobler and better quality.

Let us try to create an episode in a soap opera. Shane, a tall, dark and handsome heart-throb falls in love with Suzanne, an attractive blonde who returns his feelings. Being rather old-fashioned about these things, (as, truth be told, most young people are) they want to get married and live happily ever after.

At this point, true to soap opera tradition, we ought to introduce a snag, a thorn among the roses.

So we imagine that Shane, fine upstanding character that he is, has a tricky problem. He has seen too many marriages of his friends fall apart in bitterness and recrimination and, love

Suzanne as he does, he is nervous about whether her love for him will last. So he says to her, 'Can you prove that you will always love me?' She replies, 'I love you now, and I'll try to love you always, but I can't prove it.'

Shane's problem is within himself. He has diminished and demeaned both himself and Suzanne by asking her to prove her love. So we'll finish our episode by Suzanne giving Shane's face a good slap, and saying, 'If you can't have any faith in me – goodbye!'

In personal relationships, faith and trust are more than convenient social lubrication; there is a loftier note about them. It is much more noble to have faith in a person than to hunt around in a vain quest for proof. For faith in another person strikes a sympathetic chord of the same note, and faith is returned to us. The echoes of that faith are heard by others also, who respond in their turn, and so the quality of life in the whole community is raised.

It is this faith which, according to the New Testament, is the only way in which we can relate to God. It is when we take the facility which we use in daily life and personal relationships, and apply it to God, that we can get beyond the shores of human reason and explore the realities that lie further. There is no suggestion in the Bible that faith is somehow inferior to logic, or that it is somehow weaker or unstable. Indeed, the core meaning of the word is of firmness, reliability, and steadfastness.

But how can we begin to apply the faith we use in our everyday life to our relationship with God? The vital thing to realize is that it is a two-way process, a joint production.

Faith begins with a trumpet fanfare, with the loud, positive assertion that *God has faith in us.* This is a truth that is taken so much for granted that no-one bothers to mention it. Yet it is the starting point of it all. Psalm 46 has two sections, and the chorus at the end of each is, 'Yahweh Sabaoth is on our side.'

God creates us, sustains us, sacrifices and suffers for us, and in spite of being continually let down, still believes in *us*, and in our ability to respond to him.

It is easy in this troubled world to lose faith in each other and even, in our depression, to lose faith in ourselves. But this must be said, and it cannot be said too often - God still believes in us; there is still a road back.

Not only this, but God's faith is an active faith, and it creates resonances in us, like a piano humming in response to a similar sound in a room. When we answer, however hesitantly and uncertainly, he reinforces our little faith with his. So, gradually gathering confidence, we climb the ladder of faith, from the nervous, 'If you're there, God . . .' prayer of the first rung, to the height of praying: 'Lord, here I am; what do you want me to do?'

As the captain of a jumbo jet makes small movements in the cockpit which trigger off hydraulic and electrical motors to move the vast flying surfaces, so our small movements of faith release God's power in our lives, and he reinforces our feeble faith.

The father of the sick boy in the Gospel story has puzzled many people when he said to Jesus, 'I do believe. Help me to overcome my unbelief.' His response becomes clearer when we see that faith is a two-way process, and starts with God's faith in us.

When John Wesley was in the throes of the spiritual convulsion which started his ministry in 1738, he went to his religious adviser, the Moravian missionary Peter Bohler, and complained that his faith was too weak. 'Preach faith until you have it,' was the reply he received. Peter Bohler knew that, however small our faith to start with, God always augments it, reinforces it, and stabilizes it.

The ultimate aim is to achieve that utter and complete confidence in God that a young child has in its mother and father. Any parents know that heart-stopping moment when a youngster will launch himself off the table into thin air, so sure that dad will catch him that there's no risk at all, and it's a lovely game. It is that quality of childlike faith, heart-stopping though it may be to onlookers, that Christians aim at as they launch themselves into the unknown with a blithe disregard of the dangers.

It is, however, the quality we need. For if we are to leave the hard ground of reason and logic, and allow our pilgrimage to take us out on to the deep sea of God's paradox, then our faith must be seaworthy and strong.

3 *Dog Spelled Backwards*

What a peculiar word – GOD; a word whose derivation is even uncertain. It is dog spelled backwards, and means only what we choose it to mean.

It can mean everything, total reality, as it did to St Augustine of Hippo who described God as 'an infinite circle whose centre is everywhere and whose circumference is nowhere'.

It can mean the filling of life's gaps. It has been said that there is a 'God-shaped hole' in life, and that life doesn't add up unless we include God in our equations. As the Italian proverb puts it, 'He who leaves God out of his reasoning doesn't know how to count.'

Others use the word God to explain the spiritual experiences of their lives, like Miguel De Unamuno who said, 'I believe in God as I believe in my friends, because I feel the breath of his affection, feel his invisible hand, drawing me, leading me, grasping me.'

In the eighteenth and nineteenth centuries the word God meant a heavenly judge who ruled the world with a rod of iron. George Whitefield was, some say, the greatest preacher England has known, certainly he was the greatest preacher of the eighteenth-century evangelical revival. He worked as a pot boy at a local inn while studying as a 'poor scholar' at Oxford. His conversion took place when he was overwhelmed with a sense of his own guilt, and spent whole nights sobbing under a hedge waiting to be struck down by the fierce God he felt he had offended.

As a young minister I used to visit isolated villages for services and had to stay the weekend. I became quite expert in the Victorian furnishings, and especially the pictures, of country cottage parlours. Apart from 'The Stag at Bay', there was another picture which must have been very popular a hundred years ago, for I saw it continually. It was called 'The Road to Perdition', and was a print the size of a large poster. It showed the winding road of sinfulness, starting at the bottom with minor sins like card playing, and as the path wound upwards went from drunkenness to wife beating, theft, murder, to the ultimate horror, at the top, of 'Sunday trains'! At every curl of the path there was a bonfire where little devils were roasting the unfortunate travellers. The Victorians' understanding of God was as a judge.

It was inevitable that there should have been a reaction in our century to this fearsome understanding of God. Nowadays it is popular to stress that God is Love, for does not the Bible use these very words? Unfortunately, it all depends what you mean by love. This meaning can go too far, as well. It can get to the point where God is seen as a benevolent Father Christmas, who always spoils his children and would never, ever criticize us. It may be charming to visualize God having a wonderful time painting the butterflies, tuning the birds, polishing the clouds and chuckling as he invented voices for the ducks, but it isn't very realistic.

The word God means what we choose it to mean. This is not to say that God himself is a human invention, but that if he is a great mysterious presence who lives in paradox, the words we use to describe or name him must, of necessity, be just human conveniences. We have to call him something; but we have also to face the fact that whatever we call him is bound to be partial, one-sided, and will say as much about us as about him. In particular the words and names we use will describe our needs at the time.

The camel is a large beast with a very supercilious expression, and the bedouin have a saying to explain it. They believe that God has one hundred names but that their religion of Islam knows only ninety-nine, hence the camel's look of ineffable superiority – he knows the other one!

But one name, ninety-nine, or 999 – it would be the ultimate in human pride to imagine that any human words of ours could sum up that great paradoxical being that we call God. As the hymn-writer Faber put it:

> That Thou shouldst think so much of me,
> And be the God Thou art,
> Is darkness to my intellect,
> But sunshine to my heart.

The most we can hope for is that we may find in our fallible words and shallow thinking a few glimpses into the nature of God, sufficient to help us on our pilgrimage.

The Bible gives interesting examples of different names for God. In the early books of the Old Testament he is called by the Hebrews '*El*'. This word is one which many scholars think has the meaning 'to be strong'. A variation is *El Shaddai*, meaning 'The Almighty'. So we find many names in the Bible which include *El*, like Beth-el (the house of God).

When we consider the situation of the early Hebrew tribes, how natural it is that the quality they would want above all other in their God would be strength! They were a wandering desert people at the mercy of drought, sandstorms, and encroaching tribes of strangers who might at any moment use superior numbers to deprive them of the grass that their animals, and therefore they, needed in order to survive. Indeed, at one point in their history they were driven by starvation into Egypt where they found that their food had to be bought with the bitter price of their own liberty. This episode, and their agonizing escape from it, was a lesson the Jews have never forgotten to this day.

In that situation the overriding thing they looked for from their God was power - power to resist, power to overcome, power to foil Pharoah and escape. Were it happening today, their marching song would be 'We shall overcome'; as it was they called their God '*El*' - the Strong One.

A more modern illustration of this view of God is found in what has been called the 'national anthem of the Reformation', the hymn '*Ein' Feste Burg*', written by Martin Luther. It is difficult today to realize how vulnerable those early reformers felt, the opposition they faced, and the profound courage they needed to face it. Luther was one solitary Augustinian monk up against all the moral, spiritual, and political power of Rome, and was a citizen of a small and weak German principality which could easily be crushed. He also knew that Jan Huss of Bohemia had also protested against the abuses of Rome a hundred years before, and had been burned at the stake as a result.

Luther can have had no illusions when he nailed those ninety-five theses on the door at Wittenburg that his life expectancy would probably be measured in months, not years. That this was no idle fear was dramatically demonstrated when he had to be kidnapped by his friends and hidden in a remote castle to prevent his assassination. In this atmosphere of deadly danger he wrote the hymn that swept Germany; the hymn that sings of a strong God.

> A safe stronghold our God is still,
> A trusty shield and weapon.
> He'll help us clear from all the ill
> That hath us now o'ertaken.

There are times when every Christian has (metaphorically at least) to call God '*El*', or hum *Ein' Feste Burg* to himself.

The stresses of life, the difficult choices, the debilitating suffering – all force us to admit our own weakness and inability to cope. Fortunately, when a Christian is knocked down he's knocked on to his knees, and from there it is easier to get up because the strength of God is with us.

There was an elderly lady whose face showed the wear and worry of many crises and struggles. Yet, as her fellow churchgoers knew, she had a reason for every wrinkle, for her husband had died young, leaving her five children to bring up alone. It had been a tremendous battle, but after the last one had left home someone asked her how she'd managed it. Her eyes twinkled as she replied, 'After my husband's funeral service, and as soon as the children were asleep, I knelt down and said, "Lord, if you'll supply the grace, I'll supply the grit" – and he did.'

As the Hebrew people became stronger and more sophisticated, and as the books of the Old Testament go on, so the name *El* drops out and a new name is used, *Yahweh.* The Book of Exodus describes God appearing to Moses and saying, 'I am Yahweh, and I appeared to Abraham, Isaac and Jacob as God Almighty, but by my name Yahweh I was not known to them.' This new name came into general use when the Hebrews started to settle down to an urban farming lifestyle in their new country. In meaning it is still associated with strength, for Yahweh speaks in thunder and lightning, and guides his people with smoke and fire. He is a God of the hills, revealing himself on Mount Sinai in the North Arabian desert and coming from there to assist his people in their battles.

In view of their needs at the time, it is natural that they should still look for strength in their God, for even though by now they were much more than a wandering desert tribe, they were still a very small community squashed between great empires on both the east and west. In any argument between those early super-powers the aggressor must inevitably walk over the Israelites first and snuff out their fragile nation. In such a situation they could only take to the hills, and have as their God, a God of the hills 'from whence cometh my help'.

But there is another nuance to the name Yahweh which is worth exploring. The writer of the Book of Exodus actually defines the name when he describes how God called Moses to save his people: 'Moses said, "The children of Israel will say to me, 'What is God's name?'" And God said to Moses, "I AM THAT I AM; say that I AM sent me."'

Experts who have studied the language of the period say that the actual Hebrew words do not mean 'I am', so much as a future 'I will be'. To put it simply, the 'I am' will always be the 'I am'; God will always be contemporary, and he will always be the same, yesterday, today and forever.

If we jump forward a few centuries we reach the time of the prophet Isaiah. He was born about 765 BC, a natural 'hell-fire preacher' who felt called by God to proclaim the fall of the then two Hebrew kingdoms of Israel and Judah. While their politicians and kings twisted and turned to make political alliances either with Assyria on one side or Egypt on the other, Isaiah preached that it wouldn't do them any good. 'We're all doomed,' he said. 'We've displeased God – and we're doomed!' This was a message that didn't make him over-popular with the powers-that-were.

What saved him was that he was much more than a fire and brimstone preacher. He was also a poet of genius, and his books had a freshness of imagination, and a majesty of style that made him a national figure. As such he may have been a political disaster, but he made a tremendous contribution to how his people saw God. Isaiah saw Yahweh as strong, but also as demanding justice and faithfulness among his people.

It is this quality of faithfulness which could well provide

the clue to the meaning in the name 'The Eternal I AM'. We can visualize Isaiah looking around at the political and social structures of his day, despairing of them, and being convinced that they could not last. He must have wondered about life and what it was all for. He must have questioned whether anything existing would survive. If even the nation of God's Chosen People was to be destroyed what was going to be left? Religious man that he was, he could only find one answer – God will be left. The great 'I AM' is here now; but more important, he will be here tomorrow, and in every tomorrow to follow. Isaiah realized that one thing, indeed the *only* thing man can know for sure about tomorrow, is that God will be there saying 'I AM'. So faithfulness to God on our part is the only road to permanence.

It seems that one of the basic building blocks of human nature is the desire to make some kind of indelible mark on the world, to do something so that people will remember that we have passed this way, and not to be forgotten like yesterday's radio programme, broadcast then, and now gone. But it is not given to many to build a pyramid, a Parthenon, or a Stonehenge – and even they are stripped, blown up, or the builders' names are forgotten.

When I bought my house I (or to be more accurate, the building society) received the deeds for the small plot of land upon which it sits. My name is written as having the legal title to so many square metres of God's good earth. But how is it possible for one human being to actually *own* a bit of the world? When human life is so short, human memory so fallible, and earthly institutions so changeable, it must be both silly and arrogant to think of land giving us any sense of permanence.

At every Cup Final thousands of leather lungs roar out the most unlikely hymn imaginable, Francis Lyte's great hymn 'Abide with me', little realizing the sense of the words:

Swift to its close ebbs out life's little day;
Earth's joys grow dim, its glories pass away;
Change and decay in all around I see . . .

So much for the fleeting nature of human life and reputation. But then comes Isaiah's great vision of Yahweh, the eternal 'I AM', our only hope of permanence –

O Thou who changest not, abide with me.

Jesus was quite clear about what he called God: it was Father: no complications, sophistries, or grandiose titles – plain Father. It is a view of God that has the simplicity and strength of a sledge-hammer. The central place this idea had in Jesus' mind is often underrated. Yet from the beginning of the New Testament to almost the end (put Revelation on one side for a moment), the idea of God's fatherhood is proclaimed in such massive volume, and repeated so often that it completely colours the way Jesus saw himself, and has influenced Christian history ever since. For Jesus, fatherhood is not just one attribute of God among many, but is so central that every other attribute is seen in the light of it. So captured is Jesus by this name that he confidently argues downwards from it; 'A father wouldn't do this to his children, so neither will God do it to you.'

So, though we may see God as our strength, our permanence, and even as our judge, Jesus taught us to see each of these things as an aspect of God's fatherhood. He is a *strong* father who will help us in our struggles; a *permanent* father who will be the sure rock in a changing world; a moral father who will *judge* us in love. Jesus has warmed that great sea on which our little boats of faith are bobbing, and has brought the great paradoxical God close. The great and impersonal qualities teased out by other minds and hearts have found in his teaching an intimacy and love that is seen nowhere else.

There is a story, told by William Barclay, that a Roman emperor was once granted a Triumph – that was, permission for a victorious general to march his troops, captives and booty through the streets of Rome to the Field of Mars amid the cheering crowds of the capital. Waiting at the saluting base, on a rostrum, were his wife and children who were looking forward to seeing him after so long a time away. His youngest son was so excited that he couldn't wait for the slow moving procession to reach him so he sidled off the rostrum, ran down the side of the crowds, and tried to slip between the legs of one of the burly legionaries lining the route. But the soldier felt him, and scooped him up. 'Oy, you can't go out there,' he said roughly but kindly. 'Don't you know who that is? That's the emperor, that is.' 'He may be your emperor,' said the boy, 'but he's my dad!'

Or, to put it as Jesus did – 'When you pray, say, "Our Father" . . .'

4 *God's Fingerprints*

Suppose that I burgled your house one day when you were out. As a keen reader of detective stories I would naturally be very careful not to leave fingerprints, so I would wear gloves. I would also avoid leaving footprints, either in soft ground outside, or muddy marks on the carpets inside. I would not catch my clothing on projecting nails, eat, drink or smoke in your house, or use any tools that I could not easily dispose of anonymously. But even if I did all that, I have betrayed something about myself that is very important – my *modus operandi* as the police call it, my profession as a burglar, and my moral attitude to other people's property.

To change the illustration, suppose I gave you a picture I had painted. You would be able to judge from looking at it something of what I am like. You would be able to tell whether I am a large, colourful and dominant person, or delicate, punctilious and sensitive. You would be able to see what kinds of scenes, happy and open, or brooding and sombre, reflect my attitudes.

In a sense this is what God has done for us. He has interfered in our history, and given us a picture in the world we live in. What can we tell about him from those two things? Which brings us to Elijah – the connection is obvious as soon as you spot it.

Purely on a human level, I've always had a soft spot for dear old Elijah. The Jews had, and still preserve, a tremendous respect for him as the greatest of their prophets, expecting him to return at the end of time. Indeed, in orthodox Jewish households even today they set an extra place, or pour a big glass of wine, at the Passover meal in their homes, just in case he should turn up to be their guest. We see this veneration reflected in the strange mountain top vision described in St Matthew chapter 17. Jesus was seen by Peter and John in the company of the two great Jewish heroes long dead – Moses and Elijah.

There was also the time when Jesus took his close friends for a weekend holiday just over the border to the beauty spot of Caesarea Philippi. 'Who do people say that I am?' he asked them. They replied, most of them, with the highest compliment they could pay. 'You are Elijah,' they said.

Who was this man, and why was he regarded so highly? On the face of it he was just plain difficult! He lived rough in the desert, dressed himself in odd scraps of home-spun camel hair, ate disgusting food, didn't believe in cutting his hair, and one doubts whether he took the trouble to wash either. Deeply distrustful of cities and civilization, he only entered them in order to denounce and condemn their policies and their politicians. Altogether he was an uncomfortable character, and, let's face it, *insanitary*. One wonders what would happen in the prosperous Jewish households of this country, who carefully set a place for him at Passover, if just as they were sitting down there was a knock on the door, and Elijah appeared, noisome and scratching, saying, 'Right, where is it? I'm famished!'

Yet, in a sense, Elijah's appeal was all of a piece with his lifestyle, for he was a throwback to older days of racial and religious purity. He was brought up on the eastern side of the river Jordan where life was still in the old style and primitive. The sophisticated urban Jews saw in him an example of the 'good old days' when they were all a travelling people, when life was much harder, but simpler; when complications were blown away in the desert wind, communities were closer in their common struggle for survival and, somehow, God's voice seemed clearer. This was how they looked back at their past, for Elijah lived at a time of great social change. The travelling people had settled down on the land they had conquered, and were learning to farm, and to build. This involved not only the practicalities of wood, mudbrick and stone, but the building of the nation: new urban systems of law, order, authority, trade, and defence.

In doing this they soon realized that politics, however basic, must involve compromise, the balance of one power against another, and the cold calculation of risk. The simple black and white choices of the desert didn't help much when faced by two shades of urban grey.

The episode that triggered off Elijah's greatest moment was in the time of Ahab who, though reviled by the religious people, was one of the most powerful and statesmanlike of their monarchs. By following his father's example he had, in carefully judged battles and equally careful alliances, extended the country's borders, strength and safety. One of these treaties, which was designed to protect the main trade routes, was with the famous sea-going people of the coast, the Phoenicians. In those days, and indeed until quite recently, political alliances were cemented by family alliances, and accordingly Ahab married the Phoenician princess Jezebel. When she moved into his palace she not only brought her trousseau, but her religion of Baalism, together with 450 priests to help her in the services. What annoyed Elijah was not only that she set up the worship of Baal in Jerusalem, of all places, but that she did it, as everything else she did, with a high-handed contempt for the feelings, morality and traditions of her new people. To Elijah, what was at stake was the purity of Israel's religion and the standard of the nation's morals.

This was the reason behind the challenge that Elijah flung

down on Mount Carmel to the 450 priests of Baal. It is significant that it was on a mountain that he chose to stage this contest – the home of Yahweh, the Jewish God of the Hills. 'Build altars, put sacrifices on them, and let's see whether Baal or Yahweh can set fire to them!' The scene on Carmel is so colourful and dramatic that it has captured not only the Jewish imagination, but that of artists and composers ever since.

Yet there is a deeper meaning to it still. It can be seen as a battle between two conceptions of God. To Elijah and the traditional Jews, God was a God of history. He was *active*, leading his people through their travels, strengthening them in their battles, influencing their decisions, and in return demanding a high discipline and moral code among his people. He was a good God for a travelling people.

The priests of Baal, on the other hand, saw their god as a god of nature. Their god knew about the soil. Had they thought of it, they would have written a poem, 'You are nearer Baal's heart in a garden than anywhere else on earth.' He was responsible for the fertility of the earth, the flocks and herds, and was worshipped by different fertility rites, including sacred prostitution, and even the occasional human sacrifice.

Who would win this epic battle of the gods? History or Nature? Looking back on it from our vantage point we can see that in reality both Elijah and the prophets of Baal had half the truth, for if there is a God at all, he must be God of both history and creation, and must leave traces of his presence in both. For we cannot touch anything, or influence anything without leaving traces of ourselves and of our thinking behind us. So we can legitimately ask the question, What can we learn from history and creation about this great paradoxical God? Has he left any fingerprints on the world he has made, or dropped anything as he passes through our history?

*

Marxist historians and those affected by their thinking tell us that human history is made up of vast struggles between classes, nations and movements, and that like great juggernauts engaged in a monstrous ballet, their progression is inevitable and predictable. There is no room for God, or for the individual, in the process; if they get in the way (and they do) they have to be squashed. The great rolling tide of history cannot be stopped, or even diverted.

The Christian rejects this view, and would claim that history just isn't like that; it is full of untidiness, individuality, and odd quirks. That is because history is the sum of the histories of people – untidy, individual, quirky people. To try to impose orderly, disciplined movements upon the past is not only unrealistic, but you have to rewrite history in order to make it fit; and if there's one thing a Christian shouldn't be, it is dishonest. The play of human personality upon history is not just a mere ornament, an obbligato between the ages, or a cadenza after a century, but is the basic structure of history. People – real people, famous or infamous, known or forgotten – are the building blocks of where we've come from, where we are, and where we're going next.

Who, for instance, could imagine what would have happened in Russia had Lenin and Stalin not been there in 1917? What would have happened had Napoleon died of smallpox in his youth, or Hitler had failed in 1933? Suppose Henry VIII had succeeded in his dream of having many legitimate sons; that Cranmer had remained a humble parish priest; that Penn, Bunyan, Wesley and Wilberforce had not been born. It would be simple-minded in the extreme to think that our history would have remained broadly the same.

People are the stuff of history, and it is through them that the God of History speaks. Looking back we can see in graphic detail examples of human depravity. All the deadly sins are there, and we can often recognize with hindsight the causes of those sins, and the suffering, usually of the innocent, that resulted from them. It is when we either identify with sympathy, or recoil with abhorrence from those past lives that the God of History speaks to us.

But the past echoes not only with horror but with holiness. Frederick Beuchner describes God walking through our history and sometimes dropping his handkerchief. We call those handkerchiefs 'saints'. It is impossible to assess the influence of the books written by Bunyan, Thomas Aquinas, Julian of Norwich, Brother Lawrence, to mention just a handful of those lives the power of whose thinking has inspired whole generations.

Apart from the contemplatives, the activists of the past who spent their lives in the service of God – those who preached and healed, taught and cared, voted and battled to bring our country one step nearer to the Kingdom of God – profoundly influenced and sometimes dramatically changed the world we live in.

The God of History speaks to us, not through mass movements, but by voices in the wilderness, who became minorities, who in the end persuaded the masses. God speaks to us through individuals, and this in itself tells us quite a lot about him.

The God of Creation also gives us hints about himself through the world he has made, though not in the naive simplicity of those who would praise the rainbow and the flowers, but ignore the deserts and the greenfly.

At the end of every television programme we see the credit, 'Producer – John Smith', or whoever. It is done, presumably, for professional pride, and to get one's name known among media people. But whether the name is on the credits or not, it must be obvious to every viewer that someone must have produced it. So, though it may seem like it sometimes, even the worst programmes don't happen by themselves. They have to be based on an idea by someone, scripted by someone, staffed, resourced, researched, arranged, publicized, and transmitted. The whole effort can take hours, weeks or even years to be finally put together, and no one could possibly doubt that behind it all there must be a guiding intelligence of some sort – a producer.

This world is much more complicated than any radio or television programme; so much so that the keenest minds of our century cannot find out how it all works, let alone manipulate it. It surely must be self-evident that it cannot have happened by accident. To use the old illustration – it is impossible to believe that, however many billions of explosions there were in a printing factory, there would ever be an occasion when a complete folio of Shakespeare would drop down from the sky. The numbers involved in thinking that this world is random chance are just too big to account for the beautifully balanced system in which we live. From the miracle of design seen through the electron microscope to the wheeling galaxies, the whole thing shouts of the existence of an intelligent, ordered mind – a producer.

We also learn from this world that we are on the 'created' side of the Creator/creation relationship. We are dependent beings. It is easy for us, having in our hands all the power of modern technology (summed up, I suggest, in the ability to put a man on the moon, and invent striped toothpaste), to imagine that we are the masters of the world. We can irrigate, fertilize, and engineer biology. We can manipulate our planet into what we want to do in the short term – but only so far. Nature has a nasty habit of reminding us that we are still very ignorant, and very selfish. In a thousand different ways the world has a disconcerting habit of kicking back at us, and reminding us that we are not 'self-made men', but are dependent creations of something, or someone, else.

One of the great names in theology was Friedrich Schleiermacher, who was born in Breslau in 1768. He was so respected and loved as a preacher, theologian and philosopher that they called him 'the father of modern theology'. In his day Christianity consisted in having to accept a number of fixed doctrines as one intellectual lump, and in cold, blind faith. Schleiermacher rejected that out of hand, and emphasized that Christianity was not a body of doctrine held in the head, but a relationship with God in the heart. 'You can know God, you can feel your sinfulness, you can be filled with God's forgiveness!' The core of it, he was convinced, was a *feeling of dependence.* It is only when we feel that we have to depend on a God who is there that it is possible to love him. It is only when we are aware of how much we rely on our fellow creatures and depend on them that we can begin to love our neighbours.

Another quality we see in God's creation is that sense of mystery which we would expect from this paradoxical deity. At the frontiers of life, at the beginning or the end, we experience a touch of that unique 'otherness' which makes some people shudder, some wonder, and others pray. In the midst of life there is death, and in the midst of death there is life. To watch the birth of anything, whether flower, animal or human baby, is to be in the presence of something both miraculous and mysterious. To sit at a bedside and watch the death of someone is utterly natural and equally moving, for the same message strikes us. At the heart of things there is mystery; not just ignorance of things which clever people will eventually discover, but real paradoxical 'otherness'.

So history and nature both give us glimpses into what our God is like – though of course, nothing like a full portrait because man has warped both history and creation by his frailty, ignorance and waywardness.

St Paul was well aware of this when he wrote his first letter to the centre of the mirror-making industry in the first century. The great sea-port of Corinth was where metal mirrors were made; glass ones weren't produced until the thirteenth century, and metal mirrors were by comparison very primitive. In spite of careful craftsmanship they were not very flat and, being metal, coloured everything they reflected. For small, close-up jobs they were adequate, but for the long view they distorted everything they showed. Thinking of what God was really like, and of the ultimate realities we shall eventually see, St Paul wrote, 'Now we see but a poor reflection in a mirror, but then we shall see face to face.'

Our human history and our earthly world are only poor distorting mirrors, but at least we can see a few significant details of the one who influences our events and creates our lives. We can see the broad outline of a great paradoxical God.

5 *Strewth!*

This rather old fashioned epithet is a contraction, of course, of 'God's truth', which was an even older swear word in the true meaning of a swear – 'I swear by Almighty God to tell the truth.'

It would be a fascinating exercise to investigate the origins of the various cuss-words in the English language. 'Bloody' probably comes from 'God's blood', 'Gor blimey' from 'May God blind me'. Perhaps we only swear on the basis of the things we care about most. If this is so, it would seem that those things are religion and sex!

When we look at that rather mild expletive, 'strewth', we are transported back two thousand years to the palace of Pontius Pilate, and the so-called 'trial' of Jesus. Pilate asked what is probably the most famous question in the world when he said to Jesus, 'What is truth?'

Some writers have pictured the sophisticated Pilate asking the question as a sardonic joke that didn't deserve an answer, least of all from the Galilean peasant the proud governor-general had in front of him. Others see in the brief Bible account a much more sensitive, almost wistful man, who had thought about the question often and despaired of ever finding the answer. Whichever way it was, it is one of the piquant ironies of history that when he asked that question he had standing in front of him the man who said 'I AM the truth', and Pilate didn't recognize it when he saw it.

The chances are that the sardonic picture is right, and that Pilate, an educated man brought up in Roman and Greek civilization, would have thought about truth in a way typical of Greek philosophy. It is a definition of truth that is still held by the majority of people today. Seen in this way, truth is the actual state of affairs, as distinct from conclusions that don't add up, rumours that are unsubstantiated, or theories that cannot stand up to experiment – truth is *reality*.

This may seem so obvious that there is no point in discussing it. Whether the bulb we plant is a daffodil or a tulip can be proved when it comes up; whether our next-door neighbour is getting divorced or not, we shall find out in time. However, this view of truth can get us into some very deep water; it is by no means as simple as it looks.

Imagine three rather argumentative men standing in front of a flock of sheep on a northern hillside. They are trying to find the truth about that flock. The first man, being of an intensely practical turn of mind, counts them. 'There are twenty-four,' he says, 'and no one can deny the truth of that because I have counted them three times!'

'Ah, but that is a very inadequate truth,' says the second man, 'and in any case you may be wrong, for you don't know how many of these sheep are pregnant and we have not yet discussed the question of when a sheep is not a sheep. After lambing there might be forty-eight! What you have to do is to produce a proposition, a theory of their number that we can test after lambing time and perhaps discard. After all, Isaac Newton's theory of gravity seemed very true when he first wrote it, but has now been superseded by others. So your proposition that there are twenty-four sheep is a proposition that may be partially true, and partially false.'

At this point the third man joins in the argument. 'But even this isn't the truth about those sheep,' he says wisely. 'Surely it is not enough just to count them, for they could equally well be bananas. If they are sheep you will have to describe them as part of the genus *ovis*, and say which of the 200 breeds of domestic sheep they are. You must fit them into their place in the natural kingdom. You must also place them into their economic niche as the farmer's livelihood, and the nation's food supplies. In fact we need to see them in relation to everyone and everything else in a cosmic pattern, otherwise you're just playing with the word "sheep".'

But the first two men argue back. 'Who can possibly know enough about everything to be able to do all that? If we tried, we're as likely to be wrong as right. We could only produce a cosmic view that we *believed* to be true.'

'Precisely,' says the third man. 'Truth is a matter of faith.'

If we think of truth as reality we are bound to get ourselves into areas of abstract thought like this, and these would have been the kind of arguments in Pilate's mind.

Jesus, however, the man standing in front of him, meant quite another thing by the word 'truth'. For he had been brought up in the Jewish tradition where truth was another word for the nature of God: godliness. For a thing to be true it has to be God-like, for truth is the unshakeable substance of God. Reflecting this definition of truth, the Bible often translates the word for 'truth' with the English words 'confirm', 'sure', 'reliable' and 'valid'. In fact the word 'amen' comes from the same root. In the Psalms the eternal I AM, Yahweh, is described as 'keeping truth for ever'. The main quality of truth as the Jews saw it was that it was permanent, fixed, eternal. Absolute truth must be a basic reference point that is always the same.

A young newly married couple were given as a wedding present, not only the regulation four toast racks and impossible pictures, but one of those invaluable 'kitchen wants' boards. It was the kind that had a list of groceries and by the side of each item from 'apples' to 'yoghurt' was a slot and a sliding peg. Whenever they ran out of anything all the starry-eyed wife had to do was move the peg, and make a list of the items next time she went to the shops. Unfortunately the brand-new husband fixed the board to the back of the door. The result was that whenever the door slammed they suddenly needed everything!

The Jews knew that moral truth, and spiritual truth, needs a firm and fixed foundation. Without it, the only hope is to go with the majority and try to be slightly better than the prevailing social climate at the time, or emulate the best among our neighbours or social equals.

The Jews found their fixed foundation in their comprehension of God, and so did Jesus. This was their genius. Other people saw in their gods treachery, fickleness, cruelty, vindictiveness, and every human fault and failing. The Jews saw in their God the ultimate truth and morality; their measure of right behaviour was measured by him, and their definition of truth was God-like-ness. As they saw it, people must desire Godliness inwardly, must speak it, seek it, and walk in it. To live a *true* life one must live in unwavering conformity with God's will.

This was the vision of truth that Jesus had, and what he would have given in answer to Pilate's question had the circumstances been different. He had already hinted broadly at it when he told Pilate, 'I came into the world to bear witness to the truth, and everyone who is of the truth hears my voice.' Read the word 'God' instead of 'the truth', and the meaning remains precisely the same.

It is this view of truth that remained with the writers of the New Testament, and is still the basis of Christian thinking today. Christianity has founded its whole system of what it believes to be true upon what it understands of God's nature. Its faults have not arisen because it has done that, but because in the nature of things the Church's appreciation of the great paradoxical God has been too small and too shallow. The problem when Galileo was condemned by the Pope for saying the earth went round the sun, was that the authorities in Rome tried to answer a scientific question with theology, and were not humble enough before their God. If our conception of God were complete we should also have the answers to the problems of existence and the truth of the universe.

Probably the only proper reason anyone can have for being a Christian is because he believes it to be true. We should be Christians because we are followers of truth and not delusion. (It goes without saying that we belong to our particular churches mostly by accident.)

The Christian naturally looks to Jesus for the truth. But where is it found? In what he said? Clearly, the words, and even more, the word pictures and stories he used, have echoed down the centuries like the reverberations of a great gong. Every Christian civilization has had its language deeply affected and influenced by the words, phrases and concepts that Jesus used. This is an astounding achievement for a man who never wrote a book, travelled overseas, commanded an army, or taught for more than three years. Yet who, churchgoer or not, has been unaffected, at second or third-hand even, by the stories of the Prodigal Son, the Good Samaritan, or the Lord's Prayer? His teaching was revolutionary, progressive, on a very high spiritual level, and yet homely too. For many people, then and now, what he said is accepted as *true* teaching. And yet the centre of truth is not in what he said.

Was it, then, in what Jesus did? For words are cheap but deeds are more costly. The accounts we get of his actions in the Gospels harmonize with his teaching – he practised what he preached, and in many ways acted far beyond his words. We read of his healing of the sick, his compassion for the poor and exploited, and his great moral choices which ended in his self-sacrificial death. No one can be unimpressed and unmoved by the depth of Jesus' determination to do the will of the God he called Father. As the intervening centuries have proved, actions speak louder than words, and the vast majority of pictures painted, murals executed and statues carved have illustrated what he did, rather than what he said. Yet even though all he did was a true working out of the truth, it was not the heart of it.

The Christian sees the central core of the truth in what Jesus *was* – in the totality of his personality. When we are asked for a definition of the truth we can only point to the Gospels of Matthew, Mark, Luke and John, to Jesus the divine man, and say, 'There, in those four books, in the person portrayed there, is the nearest we can get to a definition of absolute truth.'

What Christians are in fact saying, is that Jesus' world view, the picture which Jesus spoke of, acted upon, and was consumed by, rings true for them; that what Jesus lived out respecting the world, his neighbours and God, finds an answering chord within their hearts and minds.

I once interviewed a school crossing warden for a television programme and asked him why he was a Christian. 'You are not the first to ask,' he said. 'I'm a Christian because it suits me – deny that if you can.' Apart from being a clever way out of awkward questions, he had a profound point. What Jesus shows us is the great paradoxical God translated into human terms, and operating human size. Here is God trying to fit us up with his view, like a new suit.

The writer of St John's Gospel was an educated and deep man. He was concerned that the religion of Christ should be made understandable to people outside the Jewish culture in which it was born. Fortunately he understood both Jewish and Greek thinking. He started as he meant to go on, for at the beginning of his first chapter he took the Greek idea of *logos*, meaning 'word', or 'reason'. This *logos* was responsible for the order, regularity and magnificent pattern of the world around us, and also gave to man the power to think and be rational. Every non-Jew in the civilized world knew about the *logos*, and it was to these that St John's Gospel was aimed.

So we find in his first chapter not the Jewish idea of Jesus the Messiah, which would have meant nothing to his readers, but this: 'In the beginning was the *logos* . . . and the *logos* became human and lived among us, and we saw his glory.' To the writer of the Gospel, Jesus *was* the *logos*.

When Christians try to define the truth, we see the same process at work. As we have seen, the Greeks thought of truth as ultimate reality, whereas the Jews thought of it as God-like-ness. St John puts the two together. God is the ultimate reality, he says, and Jesus the perfect human illustration of it. So in St John chapter 14 Jesus is reported as saying 'I *am* the truth.' This is putting Jesus in a unique position. Many others have spoken the truth, many people have lived it out, but only Jesus could say, 'I *am* the truth'.

This is saying to everyone who thinks of truth as reality, or as a total world vision, 'Here, in this one person, is the perfect microcosm of reality; truth is not a principle, a doctrine, or a proposition, it is a person, and here he is!' Here is not only the statement of moral perfection, not only the example of moral excellence, but perfect God-like-ness in human form – it is he that is the ultimate reality, the perfect truth.

Pontius Pilate querulously asks, 'What is truth?' while the truth about God and the world stands before him. The warp and weft of Pilate's life, as of every life, is a twisted mixture of loves and hates, humilities and prides, compassions and resentments, fears and fantasies. In Jesus we see all the emotions and moods of human life put into true proportion and priority, all wrapped in complete faithfulness to the ultimate reality – God.

Had Pilate, looking at the man standing before him for judgement, forgotten his question, and simply said, 'Strewth', he would have been morally, spiritually, and theologically absolutely right!

6 *The Inside-out Teacher*

When people put on a uniform it somehow 'sets' a relationship with other people. Whether it is a nurse's apron, a policeman's helmet, or a doctor's black bag, you know, approximately at least, where you are with them. The policeman may, in fact, be a quivering beginner on his first day, frightened of every dog that barks, but the uniform helps him and others – it defines his role.

Jesus set himself up as a travelling teacher of religion, a 'scribe', or 'rabbi' – the words were interchangeable. Everyone seems to have accepted him in this role, except the people of his own home town of Nazareth. Mary Magdalene greeted him in the Easter garden with the words, 'Hail, Teacher'; the disciples in extreme danger in a storm on the Lake of Galilee asked, 'Teacher, don't you care?'; even his enemies said, 'Teacher, we know that you teach rightly.'

Why did Jesus take on the guise of a rabbi – a teacher authorized to interpret the Jewish Law?

He would have argued, surely, that unusual, disturbing, and provocative as his teaching was, he was truly interpreting the central simple heart of the Law. Of that inner core he taught that not one dot or comma would ever be out of date. But he attacked so strongly what he saw as the perversions and misapplications of that Law, that perhaps he was afraid that people might think he was anti-Jewish, or even anti-religion. To guard against that, and to demonstrate that he was positive as well as negative, a pioneer as well as a revolutionary, he assumed the habits and traditions of a travelling rabbi.

There was a severely practical reason, too. Anyone in Palestine at that time could speak and argue privately about religion and morals; but to preach and teach in public about the Jewish Law, to expound on things like keeping the Sabbath, fasting, marriage or any of the many other applications of the Law, was strictly limited to authorized rabbis. If anyone else tried to do it they would be promptly interrupted and arrested. In contrast, an accredited rabbi fitted into a long and accepted tradition. He was welcomed into synagogues and invited to preach and teach. He was usually accompanied by a group of students who wished to follow him to learn more. The Roman occupying forces in the country were on their guard against the ever-present danger of sedition and revolt, and were very suspicious of any group which might be the core of a conspiracy against them. But a rabbi could travel and confer with his disciples free from any interference or harassment. They were a harmless part of the scenery. Roman soldiers drafted in from other countries would, no doubt, have regarded them as unusual and rather quaint local characters.

The local people also knew what to expect from a rabbi. When he sat down it was a recognized signal that he was about to teach, and they knew he would give them instruction on religion and morals, not on politics or anything else.

Being a rabbi also solved Jesus' problem of subsistence. Travelling rabbis were often supported by devout, and sometimes rich, women who, though they could not travel with them, contributed food and money. Jesus was very caustic about those rabbis who abused that generosity and took advantage of their sponsors. St Luke gives the names of some of the women who 'used their own resources' to provide for the simple needs of Jesus and his disciples. These contributions meant that Jesus could concentrate on his mission without having to do casual building work. (The treasurer was a certain Judas Iscariot.)

So we see Jesus, travelling the country as a self-appointed rabbi, fitting into a very traditional role, yet shocking the people he taught by everything he said. We can sympathize with average synagogue-goers who, mildly interested to see what this visiting rabbi was like, found themselves rocked back on their heels by him, and completely unable to fit him into any previously known category. 'The people were astonished at what he said, because he taught them with the authority of a scribe, but not with their teaching.' He sat down as rabbis did, he used parables as they did, handled subjects only they could touch; and yet what he actually *said* was dynamite!

The whole business came to a head just before the crucifixion when the chief priests in Jerusalem bluntly challenged Jesus to produce his credentials. 'By what authority do you do these things?' Jesus answered them with another question about John the Baptist, reminding them that authority in religious matters came from God, not from the priesthood.

What scandalized the religious establishment was not only his self-appointment but the substance of his message, for he turned many of the religious ideas of the day inside-out.

As against the reverence the Jews had for the 'Promised Land' they lived in, Jesus proclaimed the coming of a new kingdom, a new 'Commonwealth of God', which is not of this world, and where the priorities will be very different. Instead of the 'Thou shalt not's' of the Ten Commandments, he proclaimed 'Happy are those who . . .' The negatives were changed into positives. 'Love your friends and hate your enemies' was turned into 'Love your enemies', loyalty to your own race was turned into loyalty to all mankind. The effect of all this was as if he had strode into a synagogue on a chilly day and thrown open all the windows.

Jesus also emphasized the inner motives of what people did, not just the actions themselves, and in the Sermon on the Mount (St Matthew chapters 5–7) he gave no less than six examples. The prevailing fault of Jewish religious practice, and to be fair, of all religious practice everywhere, was to concentrate on doing all the right religious things, regardless of what the motives might be at the time.

There is a subtle distinction between a man who is determined to do the right thing even when he doesn't feel like it – a wholly admirable trait, for his motives are bound to lag behind his actions – and a hypocrite who has no intention of making his motives catch up with what he does. Perhaps the word *hypocrite* gives the clue; it was originally a Greek word used for actors in a play. The difference must lie in those who watch. The aspiring righteous man does the deed because it is right, the hypocrite does it for benefit of the audience and the applause.

A classic fictional story illustrates this point. It concerns the opening of the Cyrus Q. Smith Orphanage in America. It was opened by the man himself with these words: 'I gave a million dollars to the Cyrus Q. Smith Library, another million to the Cyrus Q. Smith Hospital, and yet another million to the Cyrus Q. Smith Old Folks Home, and I'm glad to tell you tonight that I'm giving a further million to this cause, the Cyrus Q. Smith Orphanage. And I'm going to give it, as I have done with all the others – anonymously!'

As well as underlining the value of inner motivation, Jesus emphasized the importance of ordinary people and turned the usual hierarchy of class and status on its head. Although men and women of all ranks in society were among his supporters he did not preach in the ancient corridors of power, but to the ordinary villagers and townspeople of his day. There is a record of one fleeting chance of influencing the high and mighty when Jesus said 'Follow me' to a rich ruler. He wanted to follow, but was not committed enough and reluctantly withdrew. He was 'the apostle who never was'. No doubt Jesus was sorry too, for here was a man who had the opportunity and the connections to make the message of the new Kingdom echo through the halls of Herod, and the spacious villas of the élite. But it was not to be.

So when Jesus spoke it was to artisans, fishermen, small-holders, shopkeepers and shepherds, the kind of people who just managed to keep body and soul together. In a good year they might have enough money left over for the occasional luxury, in an average year they broke even, and in a bad year they were in real difficulty – their problem was that they had no margin. When Jesus addressed this class of people he knew them well, for he was one of them himself. The pictures he drew and the stories he told applied to the world with which they were all very familiar. He talked of the man who had unexpected guests and had no spare food in the house; the woman whose entire accumulated capital was ten pieces of silver worth about one pound each, and who disastrously lost one of them.

Jesus' audiences were in general restless, anxious and discontented, and it was for that reason that no less than fourteen of his parables were about the subject that concerned them most – money.

It is interesting to look at the prayer he taught his followers. One of the phrases, 'Give us this day our daily bread,' has been a puzzle for centuries. The word translated as 'daily' occurs nowhere else in the New Testament, or indeed anywhere else in Greek literature. St Matthew was accused for a long time of making it up! Its translation into the English 'daily' was an approximate guess. But not very long ago a papyrus fragment of an ancient shopping list was dug up, and against one item on it was written this very word – it turns out to mean 'tomorrow's'. So the prayer should read, if we want to be finicky about it, 'Give us today tomorrow's bread.' This translation makes it ideal as a prayer for ordinary people who are preoccupied with where the next meal is coming from – for people on the borderline. It reminds us that we are dependent on God for our survival; but it is also a prayer for peace of mind, freedom from worry, release from the anxiety of ordinary things; time to think about the eternal realities.

In Jesus' teaching it was the poor, the exploited and the humble who, in spite of their worries, grasped the heart of what God was trying to say to them far more readily than the rich and powerful. To take one of his illustrations (and one possible translation of it), 'It is far easier for a ship's cable to pass through the eye of a needle, than for a rich man to enter the Kingdom.'

It was this appeal to the common people that ensured the spread of Christianity as fast and effectively as it did. The history of religions imposed from the top has not been a happy or effective one. What one ruler can impose another can dispose. But, carried as it was by merchants, sailors, refugees and visitors – ordinary people – Jesus' message spread like a blood transfusion through the veins and arteries of the ancient world with staggering speed. Celsus, a first-century Roman scholar and doctor, wrote a stinging attack on the early Church; 'We see them in their own houses, wool-dressers, cobblers and fullers, the most uneducated and vulgar persons. They are like a swarm of bats, frogs holding a symposium round a swamp, or worms in conventicle in a corner of the mud.'

It was exactly this appeal to the ordinary people that was, and is, the glory of Christianity. Jesus gave ordinary people value, meaning and status. St Paul said that it didn't matter whether people were slaves, freemen, Jews, Greeks, men or women; all are citizens of the new community. 'We are no longer strangers, foreigners, refugees, as we may be in this world,' he thundered, 'but fellow-citizens with all other Christians in the Commonwealth of God.'

In his teaching Jesus also swept away the whole idea of religious status, a point that was bound to antagonize the religious authorities of his day. 'Don't allow yourselves to be called "Master", "Teacher" or "Father",' he told the Pharisees who did all these things. 'You're no better than anyone else,' was what he told them. More than that, this human hierarchy of theirs was a positive hindrance to a real relationship with God.

It is interesting that at no time did Jesus allow himself to get involved in social or political concerns. This aloofness from the problems of the day perplexed the people at the time, and has puzzled Christians ever since. How could he have been so compassionate to the sick, the hungry and the poor without also protesting to the rulers who created these conditions in the first place? How could he have inveighed against the way that the religious authorities taxed the underprivileged so heavily, without seeking to change the system which imposed the taxes?

It is not a matter of opinion, but of fact, that Jesus consistently refused to entangle himself with politics; he put forward no programme, announced no schemes of reform, though he could have gained a bigger following and been very popular by doing so.

Why didn't he? There were, after all, many issues he could have supported which were in perfect harmony with the rest of his teaching.

For example, the Roman Empire was based on slavery; there were sixty million of them. In the eyes of Rome a slave was not a person but a thing – a living tool. A slave owner could throw out a slave, he could torture and even kill him for any reason or none. Slaves were not allowed to marry, and if they had children they belonged to their master and not their parents, just as a lamb belongs to the farmer and not to the parent sheep. Why did not Jesus take up their cause?

Another issue was taxation policy. Taxes were farmed out to the highest bidder and the tax-collector was expected to pay himself back that sum plus the cost of collection, through the taxes he collected. It was a system which encouraged efficiency, but it also was wide open to corruption; and tax-collectors were a byword for fraud and for the imposition of taxes over and beyond those the government required. They were notorious for being grasping, dishonest and pitiless in making their targets the poor and the helpless who couldn't fight back. Here was a cause that Jesus must have felt strongly about, and had probably suffered from personally, so why didn't he say anything in protest?

He surely could not have thought these issues, and others like them, unimportant. When we think of the Jesus described in the Gospels, the lover of mankind, wise, tender, sympathetic, it is incredible that he should not have wanted to change the conditions which brought such unhappiness and degradation to the people he loved. He appears to have simply ignored these burning questions as if they didn't exist.

In a sense that is exactly what he did. For the clue to his otherwise inexplicable silences lies in the fact that he was an 'inside-out' teacher. Jesus seems to have seen these social problems as symptoms of a deep sickness in people's hearts, and he had set himself to cure the underlying disease.

There are two ways of curing the problems of the world. The first is to tackle them from the outside inwards. 'Reshape your economic policies in order to create employment,' governments are told. 'Rethink the financial system of the world so that the developing countries can be fed,' the banks are urged. 'Abandon all weapons and spend the money on development,' good-hearted people say.

Only an idiot would decry sensible and compassionate policies like these, idealist though they may be; but unless they are backed by the *will* of the people they are just bureaucratic paperchases. Every government must in the end reflect the will of the people, and if the will is not there the machinery of change, however good, will remain idle. For it is not true that if we have perfect institutions we shall then have perfect citizens and live in a perfect world. Experiments in social engineering in totalitarian countries have usually ended in horrendous suffering and chaos. Tackling problems from the outside and working inwards doesn't seem in practice to work very well, or for very long.

Jesus worked from the inside outwards; he assumed that the only way to get a permanent cure for the problems was to start with the people involved. 'Get the hearts and wills of the people right, and eventually the institutions will come right as well,' seems to have been his approach. He appealed to his listeners to put the service of God first, to build upon the rock of godly character, 'and then all the changes in the structure of the world that you so much want will be added to you.'

Clearly Jesus stood apart from the economic and social questions of his time not because he didn't care about them, but because he did. He knew that the only way to provide a lasting cure for the deep-seated malaise in society was not by political agitation, terrorist action or passive disobedience, but by tackling the heart of the trouble – the wrong relationship people had with God.

He was well aware that to take a clear and loud stand on social issues would have made him a popular figurehead in a large mass movement. Thousands were waiting, as the Roman occupying forces were only too conscious, for a spark to light the tinder-dry discontent of the people. It is clear that

Jesus had thought long and hard about the tactic he would use during his ministry. At the beginning he had disappeared into the wilderness by himself to sort it all out. On his return he told his closest associates about the options he had considered, and did it in picture-book language that they never forgot. The temptation to lead a movement which would feed the hungry, and sort out the problems and injustices of his people, was almost overwhelming, but he turned it down because it would have distracted him and his followers from his real role. He turned away from the road of easy popularity and easy understanding.

Instead he spoke in deep, profound, and disturbing ways about the individual soul and its relationship with the great paradoxical God he called 'Father'. It was an inside-out technique, and it is working. For not only does it prepare us for 'the kingdom not of this world', but the inner dynamic of Jesus is still at work grappling with twentieth-century problems, long after the social concerns of *his* day have crumbled into history.

7 *The Upside-down Revolutionary*

By definition revolutionaries want to turn things upside-down, to 'revolve' them. It has become fashionable to see Jesus these days as a freedom fighter who went around laying an axe to the roots of the structures of his day. There is no doubt that he did preach liberty for the captives, justice for the oppressed, and food for the hungry. But in what sense did he mean it?

Looking at the Song of Mary in St Luke's Gospel which is recited so often in church by mild and gentle congregations, one is struck by its startlingly revolutionary sentiments.

> My soul praises the Lord . . .
> He has performed mighty deeds with his arm,
> He has scattered those who are proud in their inmost thoughts.
> He has brought down the rulers from their thrones,
> But has lifted up the humble.
> He has filled the hungry with good things,
> But has sent the rich away empty.

No wonder the *Magnificat* has been called 'The Christian Manifesto'.

What kind of revolutionary was Jesus? To answer this we start with a joke – for there is many a truth told in jest.

The Parable of the Good Samaritan is a joke, or at least it started off as one. So it is not surprising that it should give rise to jokes ever since.

One anti-clerical version which went the rounds a

generation ago concerned the special preacher at a church who began his evening sermon with these words: 'I am going to change my sermon tonight, and preach about the Good Samaritan, and I'll tell you why. As I was leaving the church after this morning's service to go to my host's for lunch, I noticed a poor man lying in the gutter, perhaps drunk or ill; and as I arrived for this evening's service I saw a disgraceful thing – he was still there!'

A recent adaptation of the story is a caustic attack on the Welfare State. It suggests that the Good Samaritan was in fact a social worker who went over to the wretch in the gutter, examined his injuries and said, 'Dear me, the person who did this needs help!'

In Jesus' day the classic format for jokes was 'There was a Priest, a Levite and a Samaritan . . .' just as nowadays we would say, 'There was an Englishman, an Irishman, and a Scotsman.' Jesus used the well known joke style to make a telling, and indeed, revolutionary point.

The story starts with what, to anyone brought up in a Christian tradition, is a very silly question indeed. A lawyer says to Jesus, 'Who is my neighbour?' But though it may seem stupid to us, at the time it was a serious question which raised all sorts of religious and social issues.

The background is what was called among the Jews 'The Law of God'. In essence this was very simple – 'Love God', based on 'Thou shalt love the Lord thy God' in Deuteronomy, together with 'And thy neighbour as thyself' in Leviticus. The central concepts at the heart of the Jewish view of God were admirable; they were wide, deep, and above all simple.

A great Jewish teacher of Jesus' day, Hillel, was once challenged by one of his students, who promised to become a Jew provided that he could learn the Law while standing on one leg. Hillel replied with what was virtually the 'Golden Rule': 'What is hateful to you, don't do to your fellow. This is the great foundation, the rest is commentary. Now go and learn!' The words of the texts which could be summed up as 'Love God and love your neighbour', were written, carried, worn on the person, and generally revered as the heart of the matter. When rightly interpreted and followed they set a noble and lofty standard of religion, free from formality, and demanding a deeply personal relationship with God.

However, the snag lies in the words 'when rightly interpreted', for this opens the door to theological bureaucracy. By degrees this simplicity was elaborated into a comprehensive and artifical code. We can almost hear under-employed temple officials whose zeal was greater than their commonsense saying, 'What about the poor ignorant shepherd? We must give him some very simple down-to-earth rules so that he can tell whether he's loving God or not – and while we're at it, let's do some guidelines to show him how to love his neighbour.'

Eventually the simple and majestic 'Love God and love your neighbour' was elaborated into 613 'Commandments of the Law', and these in turn were subject to 'interpretation'. By the time of Jesus these rules were rigid and often absurd. For example, it was lawful to put a bandage on a wound on the Sabbath, but not to put ointment on it, because in that case the wound would heal, and that was working on the Sabbath day. Various groups of rabbis had a wonderfully enjoyable and on-going debate as to what should be done with an egg which a wicked chicken might misguidedly lay on the Sabbath. Some argued that, as the chicken was obviously depraved, to eat the egg would clearly profane the holy day; others would have gone to the synagogue on the egg and hang the consequences!

Among this welter of rules and regulations a considerable number were naturally concerned with a Jew's relationships with others. First he had laws to regulate his relations within his family, then others concerned with his neighbouring Jews. Separate rules applied to strangers, particularly regarding hospitality to folk who might be in his household at festival times. Toward the gentiles he had precious few duties at all; indeed it was even illegal to help a gentile woman in childbirth.

In order to sort out what he had to do for each group, the Jew had to be told *who* was *what*: the groups had to be defined. Not that there was much difficulty with the word 'neighbour'. There were no scattered farmhouses or isolated homesteads in the agricultural areas of Palestine. People went out to the fields from the villages and towns, which were self-contained in their own community life. Developed from early bedouin encampments, they had become settled and even fortified for the common safety of the inhabitants. The link between neighbours was very strong, the houses were very close; they borrowed, worked, argued, sang and generally lived in each other's pockets. Anyone who considered buying a house in the village would, if he had any sense, first ask the question 'What are the neighbours like?' In that society it was quite clear who your neighbours were because you knew them very well indeed.

Having looked at the background we can return to the Good Samaritan story. Jesus described a priest coming down the road and spotting the injured victim lying on the side of the road, beaten up and bleeding. He went over to him, *and saw that he didn't know the man.* He was obviously not his neighbour, so he walked on.

Notice the point that he would have walked on with a perfectly clear conscience. He had no religious or legal duty to the man; it was up to his neighbours to help him. We would have felt ashamed of ourselves, but that is because we are imbued with Jesus' teaching; but the priest would not have felt critical of himself or open to the criticism of others.

Then the Levite comes along, representing the tribe who had held hereditary posts as subordinate ministers at the Temple since the first Levites helped Aaron. He goes over to the battered casualty, doesn't recognize him as a neighbour either, and, humming the latest Psalm to himself, walks on.

The story in the Gospels is very brief and terse; the stories as Jesus told them must have been full of colour and drama. We can justifiably picture Jesus enlarging on all the characters, portraying the man in the gutter saying, 'Fine lot you are! Here I am, leaking all over the place, and all you can do is ask me to prove my identity!'

Then over the hill comes the Samaritan, one of the race that the Jews hated most. They were a racially mixed foreign lot, who had been moved into the country when Assyria conquered and transported away the ten tribes of Israel. Not only were they impure racially, but they were religiously mixed as well – half Jewish and half pagan. Most Jews would have much preferred any honest foreigner to these mongrels on their doorstep. The relationship between the two peoples was a long history of bitter enmity, broken by outbursts of general treachery and hostility. Even Jesus told his disciples not to go into Samaritan cities for fear of the uproar it would cause.

So we see coming down the road a man whom no one would have anything to do with; and yet, ironically, if anyone would help the beaten-up traveller *it had to be the Samaritan.* For the Samaritan was not bound by the rules and regulations that stopped the others from helping; he was free to allow his natural compassion to dictate what he did, and at long last the injured man received help.

What Jesus was saying in parable form was that the Jewish religion had gone drastically wrong. The original simplicity had been turned into a legalistic morass of regulations that at best obstructed and hid the real spiritual heart of their faith, and at worst actively denied love of God and love of neighbour. The message of the parable is a complete overturning of centuries of religious tradition and law, a message which, preached straight, would have ended Jesus' ministry sooner than it did. But he proclaimed it in such a way that it was very difficult for anyone to pin down. It was hard, even in those days, to sentence someone for a serious crime on the evidence of a story, even less for one that had the format of a joke.

So we see in this parable an indication of how revolutionary the teaching of Jesus actually was. He would keep and command the simple centre of the Jewish Law in so far as it brought people nearer to God and his will, but he would have no patience with anything that stood in the way of that relationship.

His standards were not those of ordinary respectable tax-paying people. In many ways his standards were much higher - impossibly high, some think - and in other ways he scandalized people with much lower standards. His priorities and criteria were just *different*, for he insisted on turning people's attitudes upside down. The priest in all his sanctity was wrong, and the despised Samaritan was right. Jesus felt himself to be the first citizen of a kingdom with a very different order of merit than obtains in our society. It would be a commonwealth where 'the first shall be last and the last first', where the top table would be occupied not by the powerful and the pushy, but by the kind of people he thought of in what we call the Beatitudes.

Let us imagine the kind of top table Jesus had in mind. That man sitting first on the left and sipping his drink looks far too ordinary to be in such an important place. We must assume that there are hidden depths to him, and we would be right. The Greek and Aramaic words used for 'poor' in the text mean not just ordinary lack of resources, but utter destitution. He is a man who has been through what Bunyan called 'The Valley of Despond', has seen the hell of meaninglessness and tasted despair. While there, he realized his own spiritual helplessness. He is completely attached to God, for he has proved that only from God can he receive the help, hope and strength he needs.

On the other side of him we see the second guest, who has lines on her face that show sorrow. She is sensitive to all the tragedy and suffering in the world, and her heart has gone out to everyone involved. But she has found that there is a limit to how much vicarious suffering one person can take without the heart breaking. Not only this but, perhaps because of it, she has become very aware of her own shortcomings; she wants to be more unselfish than she is, more caring, more loving. She mourns not only for others but for herself. But her saving grace, which saves her from being miserable company for the other guests, is the strange joy she gets from knowing that she is worrying about the right things.

Next to her, just being served with the soup, is a big man, a seventeen-stone giant looking as if he's carved out of raw beef. He's the kind of 'uncle' figure everyone likes – controlled, calm, capable. Only once has he been known to be very angry, and that was with someone ill-treating a child. He never minds what he does; if a job needs doing he'll see to it, even if he has to do everything himself. He wouldn't like to be called 'meek', but he is. He'll survive, too. For the lions, tigers and eagles of life usually end up as endangered species, while it is the sheep, cows, and pigeons which multiply.

Next to him, looking at the menu, is a lady who has a steely look about her. She is an utterly determined person who has, if the truth be told, been called a fanatic. Luckily her fixation has been on doing what God wants, not on the rigidity of a written code, or the abstruse arguments of an academic doctrine. What has saved her from humourless unattractive-ness is her determination to be joyful, charitable and loving.

Of course she realizes that in the end these qualities must flow out of her naturally, and she's working at it.

So it is just as well that she is chatting to the man opposite her who is the perfect example of human warmth. He is the sort of man everyone talks to because one never feels that he is judging or criticizing. He's been called 'as soft as a brush', and his friends know that he has a heart as big as a bucket. He's listening, really listening, which is what he does most, and best. When he listens, people feel that he understands not only what they have done, but why they have done it. He knows what makes people tick when most others only know what makes people explode, and he's the perfect shoulder to cry on.

This side of him is a young girl who is the picture of wide-eyed innocence. In a world of double meanings and subliminal messages she is utterly straightforward. She always believes people, always trusts them, and has been called naive as a result. But to listen to her is to be transported to a simpler, cleaner and better world.

Next to her, the tired-looking man fiddling with the salt cellar has the most worried expression on the whole table, for he has spent his life preoccupied with the arguments and quarrels of others. He has been the 'honest broker' in disputes without number and as a result has suffered from criticism from every side. It has, in truth, been hurtful to him, but he has carried on being the original 'battered liberal'. He knows too much for his own peace of mind of the capacity of mankind for self delusion, irrational argument, and selfish prejudice.

At this end of the table there is a woman who is bubbling with joy and who can hardly stop chattering. If you noticed when she sat down, she did so with great care, for she has a twisted back. She comes from South America, as we notice from her different complexion, and she has suffered imprisonment and torture for speaking out on behalf of the poor people in her village. To be in such a large company of people who think as she does, and to have good food and a safe future is such a release for her that she will be fizzing with excitement for a good while yet.

As we look around at the top table at the heavenly banquet, there is one encouraging thing - the guests are not all the same; indeed, they are widely different. But they each have one of the qualities demanded by citizenship in the Commonwealth of God. It was these virtues that Jesus made his priorities when he told the profound joke of the Good Samaritan.

8 *A Picture Book Saviour*

Some people find intense religious meetings, especially those of the revivalist type, rather embarrassing. There often comes a point in the proceedings when someone stands up to give what they call 'a testimony' – an account of how Jesus has 'saved' them. I must admit that this sometimes makes me squirm, and I cannot escape from the unworthy suspicion that they tend unconsciously to exaggerate their previous sinfulness in order to highlight their present 'saved' condition. An old rhyme put it well:

> Once in a saintly passion
> I cried with desperate grief
> 'O Lord, my heart is full of guile,
> Of sinners I'm the chief.'
>
> Then stooped my guardian angel
> And whispered from behind,
> 'That's vanity, my little man.
> You're nothing of the kind!'

I find it vaguely uncomfortable to hear people in public talking about the most personal relationship they have – with God. It is a bit like hearing someone talk about their second most personal relationship, between them and their husband or wife. In the right place, and to the right person, one would talk about these things, but not in public. Preaching the principles is one thing; exposing one's inner life to strangers is quite another.

However, overstated as it may be in some instances, we cannot escape the *fact* of sin, evil, tragedy, waywardness – call it what you will. There seems to be a warp in life, in the world, and especially in human nature. It is always so much harder to be good than to be bad. Our lives do not run straight like tenpin bowls, but curve like crown green bowls; we are biased in ourselves, and by the ground over which we travel. Who knows where it comes from? Theologians have blamed Adam, Adam blamed Eve, and Eve blamed the snake!

But we cannot deny the fact. Look anywhere in society and we see the calculating selfishness of the rich, the arrogant selfishness of the terrorist, and the callous selfishness of the idealist. No one can escape the mourning of the bereaved, the mute appeal in the eyes of the starving, and the anger and fear in the hearts of ordinary men and women. Sin, for let us call it that for convenience, cannot be swept away, papered over, or ignored – it has to be *faced*.

This world is not a fair world. We would all wish that the brightest and best people should receive recognition and reward, while the wicked and worst should get their just deserts. But it does not work out like that; so often the good die young, the criminal finds that crime pays, and this offends our sense of natural justice. The single parent trapped in her poverty, the purposeless teenager driven to the suicidal solace of drugs, the redundant man who has lost his identity, self-respect, and income, all ask the question: 'Why? Why should this happen to me?'

If I thought that Christianity preached a gospel that the world was just and fair, that faith was a sort of insurance policy against anything dreadful happening to us, I would not expect any one to believe me when I talked about it. Not only that, I would not believe it myself, for it flies in the face of the evidence of our own eyes. Unjust rewards and undeserved suffering come to good and bad alike, and it is foolish to pretend that they don't. I would sooner walk barefoot to an honest hell, than ride to a dishonest heaven that ignored sin and suffering.

Fortunately for Christians, Jesus saw the human condition as it really is, took seriously the world as it really is, and planted a cross in it – right in the middle.

For if ever there was an example of undeserved and unjust suffering, it is hung upon that cross. Jesus, the most perfect reflection of a great paradoxical God, was rushed through a kangaroo court and manipulated into one of the most painful deaths known to man.

The most amazing thing about it was that he was not only 'set up' by the authorities, but he knowingly and deliberately set himself up. He went voluntarily to his death, ignoring the warnings that friends sent him, because he believed it was what God wanted him to do. He believed that in some strange way his death would benefit the world.

Jesus is described in the New Testament as a carpenter. Pictures of him in the carpenter's shop usually show him as planing a beautiful piece of mahogany with a few symmetrically curled shavings carefully placed around him – not at all like a real carpenter's shop with its sawdust, dirt and cobwebs. Apart from that, most carpenters of that day worked in the open air, and in any case the word used is *tekton* which means, not cabinet-maker, but builder. A master builder was an *architekton*, from which comes our word 'architect'. Jesus was by trade a jobbing builder whose main material was wood, but who also worked in stone and mud brick. There are proofs of this in the stories and illustrations he used in his teaching. Nowhere does he use cabinet-makers' terms. One could imagine him saying something like, 'When you speak, be like a carpenter; measure twice before you cut once.' But he didn't. In contrast, many of his analogies are about building. He referred to people who built towers without first getting an estimate, and houses built on good and bad foundations. When he talked about the labour of starting a new vineyard he didn't mention the new vines themselves, but the building work involved – the putting up of a palisade, and the digging of a pit for the wine-press. He looked at Peter, heard his profession of faith, 'You are the Lord', and said that on this rock he, the builder, would build his church. Jesus was a jobbing builder, the sort of man you would call round if there was a problem with the roof, walls, or even a door sticking. He was one of those invaluable, multi-capable, jacks of all trades.

Jesus was also a northerner. The Palestine of those days was split between the fertile, relatively prosperous north, where the people were warm-hearted, impulsive and enthusiastic, the perfect example being Simon Peter; and the arid, infertile south where the people were haughty, reserved, and religiously intolerant. There was no love lost between the north and south; the southerners of Judea regarded the northerners of Galilee with contempt, and the northerners resented it! Although both spoke Aramaic, they had different accents, and Jesus and all his disciples except one had a strong northern 'twang', the one exception being Judas Iscariot (man of Kerioth' – in the south). This explains many of the hidden sneers of the New Testament. 'Are you also from Galilee?' is an insult when seen against the historical background. It also explains why Simon Peter was so easily recognized when he tried to be an unseen listener at Jesus' trial.

So, having looked at the outward character of Jesus and the place where he lived, we can ask ourselves the question: 'How can the voluntary death of a jobbing builder turned travelling rabbi, two thousand years ago and two thousand miles away, do anything for *us* here and now?' How is it possible for that act, however incredibly noble, to have any effect on the sinfulness of the twentieth-century world?

Here we must admit that again we are in the presence of a paradox. The Cross of Jesus has had an effect, and still does affect us, but by no form of logical thought can we discover *how* that effect operates. The answer is as wide as the vision of God, and as deep as his loving nature, and it is hardly surprising that we cannot understand either it or him. After all, a God small enough for us to understand wouldn't be big enough to be worth believing in.

But that has not stopped wise and holy men from trying to make some kind of sense of it. The first were the writers of the New Testament.

When we study the Bible we find after a while that it is not a book of history, politics or poetry, though it contains all these things; nor is it even a book of systematic theology – it is a picture book. The Bible bombards us with a succession of word pictures in mixed-up order, each one illustrating something of the truth of God. Given that God is greater than words, it is as good a method as any. Were the Bible to contain just one vast panoramic picture, we should be in danger of pushing the analogies too far and into extremes. But by using a whole gallery of pictures, each giving separate insights, we are expected to balance the views portrayed in them all and reach our own vision of what the truth looks like. The Bible illustrates, but does not explain.

The Gospel writers found the same problem as the prophets, and reached the same solution. Despairing of trying to explain the Cross, they illustrated with word pictures to try to shed some light into the question, 'How does the Cross save us?'

The first picture is of a law court. We are in the dock; the people we have injured by our selfishness are the witnesses for the prosecution; and on the bench is God the Judge. All sinfulness is not only an offence against those we have injured, but primarily an offence against the law, God's Law. As he is a supremely moral and just person, the justice of God must be done, and be seen to be done. So we are 'for it'! Then Jesus steps forward, and volunteers to take our place. The judge agrees, and sentences him to death so that justice may be done. St Paul was keen on this picture and drew upon Isaiah who wrote: 'He was pierced through for our faults, crushed for our sins. On him lies a punishment that brings us peace, and through his wounds we are healed.' Justice demands death, and God provides a substitute.

This is not as unfair as it might appear, for we are not shown the picture of an oriental tyrant who demands blood whether it is innocent or guilty; but if we believe that Jesus is in a sense part of God himself, it is the judge himself who has accepted the punishment. Yet even so, many feel instinctively that there is something not right about the innocent accepting the punishment of the guilty, and we cannot push this picture too far.

A second picture is of a kidnap or hi-jack. By our waywardness, we have put ourselves into the power of the devil, who directs all that we do. Jesus opens negotiations to get us released, and in the end the terms are agreed; Jesus will put himself into the devil's power on condition that he releases us. This is agreed, and as soon as Jesus is vulnerable, the devil arranges for his minions to crucify him in the hope of getting rid of God forever. St Mark put it this way: 'The Son of Man did not come to be served, but to give his life a ransom for many.'

Dramatic as it is, this picture suggests that the devil is remarkably stupid. We can also hear echoes of the Ring Cycle, and cosmic battles between pagan gods.

A third picture is based on the Jewish sacrificial system of the time, and was used by St John and St Peter. The sacrificial attitude of Jewish religion was a sophisticated and profound concept, distasteful though it is to us today. The worshipper would bring, say, a lamb, into the temple. He would lay his hand on it to show that he had identified himself with the animal. It would then be killed, and the blood taken by the priest into the presence of God in the holy place, representing the surrendered life of the worshipper. So God and the man were reconciled. But that was not the end, for the body of the animal was burnt on the altar, and the rising smoke symbolized God's acceptance of the offering. And last, the flesh of the animal was shared in a ritual meal, showing that reconciliation between God and man also means reconciliation between man and man; all the worshippers became one people praising their God.

Notice that there is no idea of punishment in this; it is a service of devotion and self-sacrifice. This practice of religion was entirely familiar to Jesus and the early disciples who were all Jews, so it was natural that in trying to make sense of the Cross they should use this sacrificial picture.

In some places they describe Jesus as the sacrifice, 'the Lamb of God who takes away the sin of the world'. If we lay our hand on him we shall be identified with him, and through his death we are put into a right relationship with God. In other parts of the New Testament Jesus is portrayed as the High Priest as well as the sacrifice: 'Christ came as High Priest . . . and entered the most holy place once for all by his own blood.'

There is little doubt that this is how Jesus himself thought of his self-giving, for after his last meal with his followers he instituted a simple and most moving ceremony. He handed round the plainest thing on the table, the bread, and said, 'This is my body, given for you,' and then the simplest drink, the wine; 'This is my blood, shed for you.' Again we see the upside-down paradox of the simplest things being used as symbols for the most precious. Then, as a personal request to his closest friends, he touchingly asked, 'Whenever you meet again, do this, and remember me.'

We have looked at three pictures of how the Cross could have worked. All of them show us something, none explains it all. Since New Testament times, holy and profound minds have puzzled over it. Some have thought of new ways to explain it, and have drawn new word pictures. All have shed fresh rays of light; none has provided complete illumination.

In the end, the Cross is a fact that cannot be explained, a phenomenon that defies description. It is as mysterious as the action of a paradoxical God is bound to be. That Christ died to save us from our sins is a fact that cannot be logically argued, but becomes blindingly real when seen with the eyes of faith.

Nearly three hundred years ago, in an art gallery in Düsseldorf, there hung a picture of the crucifixion, the *Ecce Homo* of Sternberg. The title under it read, 'All this I did for you. What have you done for me?' A wealthy young man who was on the usual tour of Europe wandered in, and sat before the picture entranced. Hour after hour he sat there with his eyes riveted to it. At closing time the caretaker had to persuade him to leave, and a dramatically changed young man went back to his inn. He was Count Nicholas Von Zinzendorf, who from that time devoted himself to the founding of the Moravian Missionary Society, whose missionaries were instrumental in the conversion of John and Charles Wesley; and a great spark of religious revival both in England and America soon roared into a blaze.

Looked at with the eyes of faith, the Cross changes lives. Somehow or other, this tremendous act on the first Good Friday cleanses us from guilt and reconciles us with our Maker.

Though some people's voices are only good enough for use

in case of fire, or for augmenting grief at funerals, most can sing if they took the trouble to learn. Then they would find the indescribable pleasure of singing in a vast choir Handel's 'Hallelujah Chorus' or Haydn's 'Achieved is the Glorious Work'. It is an unforgettable sensation, for the sound washes over you like a great wave sweeping you into a sublime paradise. It would be entirely fitting if the centre of Christian worship should be in moments like that. But the strange thing is that the deepest human needs are satisfied, not with an oratorio, or a symphony orchestra, an engraving by Dürer, or a sculpture by Michelangelo: but through a cross. We are lifted to heaven by two simple pieces of wood at an angle to each other. We find our rest with the symbol of a barbarous execution. And we discover our joy in agonizing self-sacrifice.

Looked at from the Christian point of view, some ages in the past have been light and some dark. But on that simple cross, where a jobbing builder died two thousand years ago, there was focused the white-hot point of God's love and light.

9 *The Back-to-Front Surprise*

For the first five hundred years after Christ no one bothered to celebrate the Resurrection at Easter; the day was celebrated like any other Sunday. Eventually Pope Vigilius decreed that the suitable passages from the New Testament should be read at the services, and felt that this was quite sufficient. Easter was, after all, a pagan festival, which in England was named after Eostre, an Anglo-Saxon goddess to whom special sacrifices were offered every spring. The business of Easter eggs, chicks and daffodils would have been greeted by His Holiness with an eloquent sniff.

It was not that he and the early Christians thought that the Resurrection was unimportant; on the contrary, it was so vital to their faith that they celebrated it every week, not just once a year. Indeed, the main reason for Christians choosing Sunday as their holy day, and not Saturday like the Jews, was because the Resurrection happened on a Sunday. This was emphasized by a second appearance of the Risen Christ, and the coming of the Holy Spirit, also happening on Sundays.

The early pioneering Christians thought of worshipping together on Sundays as a weekly renewal, a personal resurrection of the spirit every seven days. Whatever happened on that first Easter Sunday had a dramatic effect on Jesus' followers.

But what was it that happened? We can read the Gospel stories carefully, for all four go into considerable detail as one would expect for such a mind-boggling event, and still be confused. The stories give details concerning where Jesus' followers were, what they felt like, what they did, and what they saw, or thought they saw. The Bible also goes into the theory of why God did it; but nowhere can we find a clear, scientifically acceptable account of what actually happened in that tomb. It is frustrating for the modern mind, but to state the problem is to answer it; clearly the Gospel writers lived before the scientific method was invented. But even if they had had the benefit of our modern approach it would not have helped, for they *didn't know* what had happened – it was as much a mystery to them as it is to us. One thing is clear, the New Testament cannot explain the Resurrection of Christ.

How accurate are the stories anyway? Although scholars still argue about it, most people would accept that we can be fairly sure of the broad outline of what happened. The first Gospel to be written was that of St Mark, about AD 65, just thirty years or so after the event, well within living memory. St Mark was a disciple of St Peter when he was in Rome, and after St Peter's martyrdom, Mark was asked to write down all the stories of Jesus that Peter had told and preached. This must have been easy for him, for he must have heard these stories from Peter, the eye-witness, many, many times. We are told that Mark wrote down these stories, 'though not in any particular order'.

So unless St Peter made the whole thing up, and we know he didn't do that from the corroborative evidence in the other Gospels, we have in Mark an account straight from first-hand. Of course, some of the details may have become hazy in Peter's memory, and Mark may have made some small errors in writing it down, but there was no time for legends to grow, or opportunity for fanciful stories to spread; there were still too many eye-witnesses still living. When we weigh it up, there is better and sounder evidence for the first Easter Sunday than for almost any other event in ancient history.

We know, for example, that there was one, and possibly

two, of Jesus' supporters among the Jewish court that condemned him. Plucking up their courage, they begged the body from Pilate, and Joseph of Arimathea put it in a new tomb that he had made in his garden for himself. It was a high quality tomb, as one would expect of an upper-class man, with the usual circular stone for a door. The unusual thing is that it was a new tomb, for normally bones would be collected from a tomb after a while, and the tomb be re-used repeatedly. Those who enjoy symbols would see in the fact that Jesus was laid in a new tomb the sign of a new age, a new start, a new kingdom, rising from a new tomb.

The Gospels also agree that what astonished the visitors early on the Easter morning was that the massive stone that sealed the doorway had been rolled aside. As Mark tells us, it was a huge great thing, as big as a cartwheel, much more than three women could handle. This led them, and at first leads us, to the obvious conclusion that a group of people had got to the tomb overnight and stolen Jesus' body. But who? Certainly not Jesus' friends and followers; they were as mystified as anyone else. Neither could it have been the Roman or Jewish authorities, for they were deeply embarrassed by the rumours of the Resurrection and could easily have countered them by producing the body from wherever they had put it; but they didn't because they couldn't.

Which raises the other possibility – that Jesus did not really die, but revived in the tomb and got out by himself. This does not bear examination either; for not only is it a gross slur on the competence of a professional Roman execution squad, but the stone was heavier than one man, let alone an injured one, could move, and absolutely impossible to do from the inside.

Then we read of Jesus appearing to his followers, sometimes in small groups, sometimes in large, sometimes indoors, sometimes outside, sometimes recognizable, sometimes not – it is all very mysterious, and the Gospel writers don't know what to make of it all. The latest fashionable theory is that these appearances were all 'hallucinations', but this does not help, because if something divine caused the hallucinations, it still doesn't explain it. If they were just natural phenomena it seems very coincidental that they should happen at the same time as a great spiritual surge of power among the early Christians.

In spite of attempts by people who have wanted to attack the Church, and by Christian people who have tried to find a scientific justification for their faith, to explain the Resurrection away – sometimes to their satisfaction, sometimes not – the stories still resist an easy answer. Most people approach them with common sense, and realize that many of these new theories demand as much of a jump of faith as is required to accept that the Resurrection happened, and with much less supporting evidence. After all, if we start from the supposition that the Resurrection could not have happened, and that any Gospel statement supporting Christianity must be suspect, it is hardly surprising if we end with a different conclusion.

Whereas if we start from the position that the great paradoxical God intervened in human affairs at that new tomb, and that the Gospel writers were merely trying to tell the truth, we end up with the tantalizing conclusion that something very remarkable did occur, but that we cannot explain it any more than the New Testament can.

However – and this is the upside-down nature of it – though the New Testament cannot explain the Resurrection, the Resurrection *can* explain the New Testament, for without it there wouldn't have been one.

The most trained and educated Gospel writer seems to have been a doctor, St Luke. At the beginning of his book he mentions a surprising fact that has intrigued scholars ever since: 'Seeing that many others have undertaken to draw up accounts of the events that have taken place amongst us, I in my turn . . .' At the time when he was writing, about AD 70, he says 'many' more books were in hand or in circulation. But whose? And where are they now? We know of only two, perhaps three: St Mark's account which appeared five years before, St Matthew, who wrote at the same time as Luke; and it is also possible that St John was putting pen to paper as early as that, but the experts are still arguing about it. There also might have been a book of 'The Sayings of Jesus', which has completely disappeared. Who could have written it? It is a fascinating speculation to wonder why Jesus asked Matthew, one of the hated tax-gatherers to join his followers. Was it because, distrusted and disliked or not, Matthew had a skill Jesus needed – he could write? Perhaps Jesus wanted someone who could write down his teachings as they were given so that they could be passed on to future generations. If so, was the 'Sayings of Jesus' book, of which the only traces are preserved in Luke's and Matthew's Gospels, originally written by the young Matthew at the time? We shall probably never know the answer, but it is a captivating thought.

But whichever way it was, many books were being written, probably most of them burned by official persecution squads or lost in some other way, and one is bound to ask why the writers bothered. If the Resurrection had not happened, one would expect there to be a lofty, philosophical compendium of the speeches of a profound teacher unjustly done to death, to be handed round to interested people. Perhaps there might have been some theological enthusiasts who would treasure and study it; but the book would have been non-active, as dead as a book of Socrates, or Plato. In any case there would have been no need for more than one book, one version to keep the students happily arguing.

Instead, we find Christian seafarers, merchants, travellers and refugees crossing and criss-crossing the known world, planting small cells of Christian people with a burning missionary zeal. They were not satisfied with a brief digest of what Jesus said; they wanted to know what happened, and they heard it by word of mouth from, if they were lucky, people who were there. Had it not been for these people and their converts saying, 'Now that the eye-witnesses are beginning to go, let us have some permanent record of what they saw', the Gospels would not have been written. Had the Resurrection not happened, those people would not have been there, their converts would not have existed, and the demand would not have arisen.

St Paul had a bewildering conversion experience on the road to Damascus which he described to his dying day as an appearance to him of the Risen Christ. All his incredible journeys and sufferings would not have taken place, and all the letters he wrote, many of them now in the New Testament, would not have existed, had he not been convinced that 'if Christ has not been raised, then our preaching is useless and your believing it is useless.' He wrote this, incidentally, a mere twenty years or so after the event of the Resurrection; he was probably in Jerusalem at the time, or at least must have heard the accounts of that day from the people who were on the spot.

The very existence of the whole New Testament, Gospels, Acts, Letters and all, can only be explained in the light of the Resurrection; no other cause would have been powerful enough. Neither cynical fraud, naive wish-fulfilment, or lofty self-persuasion are sufficient to explain the existence of the New Testament; only something as incredible and startling as a resurrection would have been enough.

We have seen that the Gospels do not help us understand the Resurrection, so it would be natural to assume that the rapidly growing community of Christians would have sorted it out. But no. It was certainly an important *fact*; indeed, they went so far as to say that there were only two things one needed to accept for salvation, Jesus as Lord, and the Resurrection. But when it came to explaining what the Resurrection actually meant, they were as confused as anyone else. Matthew, Mark and Luke, as we have seen, just give the facts as they know them. St John also describes what happened, but confesses his ignorance when he says that those who believe in Christ will be resurrected like him. (This inevitably raises the question of how the unsaved unbelievers get resurrected. How do the goats get to join the sheep at the Last Judgement?)

St Paul grapples with the subject but in the end has to resort to word pictures: the resurrected body is like a grain of wheat dying and sprouting again in the spring; it is like living in a permanent building after living in a tent. But there are some general principles everyone is agreed on.

1 That Christ was resurrected in some mysterious way is a *fact*.
2 It demonstrates that you can put love and goodness in a grave but they won't stay there; in the end, love is stronger than hate, goodness stronger than evil.
3 It shows that the paradoxical God behind the world is stronger than death.
4 It guarantees that those who share Jesus' ministry will share in his victory, those who die with him will be raised with him.

This is quite enough for ordinary people to live by, though not enough to satisfy the scholars. To go beyond this would be pure speculation. So after two thousand years the Church has to admit that it has in the Resurrection a mystery that is beyond explanation, and a paradox that is beyond words.

However, as we have seen, though the Church may not be

able to explain the Resurrection, the Resurrection certainly explains the Church. The early disciples were beaten and demoralized men and women. All their high hopes and deepest desires were taken down by Joseph of Arimathea and put into a tomb. They were also very frightened. Peter was last seen at the trial; one had run away leaving his clothes behind; the rest were conspicuously absent – all except one, the youngest, who joined Jesus' mother, his aunt, Mary Magdelene, and the other women who had been his sponsors during his ministry, at the site of the execution.

They were not expecting any good news, and met on that Sunday morning because they didn't know what to do or where to go. They were miles from home, and their leader, their future, and their way of life had all gone in one disastrous week.

The contrast with what they were like a few weeks later is startling: suddenly adventurous, positive, and so confident in talking to vast crowds that bystanders thought that they were drunk. Far from being a last spasm of despair, this audacious spirit spread down the years and over the Roman Empire, driving the early Christians to incredible feats of travel, teaching, suffering, and some even to a martyr's death. In spite of vicious persecution when communities were scattered, books burned, and lives lost, those early Christians spread like fire through stubble. Something very big must have started it all. Deny the Resurrection, and we should have to invent some other cause for this sudden change.

We have looked at the evidence from the empty tomb and the rolled-aside stone, but the most convincing evidence of all is the Church itself; for without the Resurrection the Church would not have begun to exist, and certainly not spread as widely and as quickly as it did.

To take a parallel example: the actual contemporary manuscript evidence that William of Normandy beat Harold at the Battle of Hastings is thin, as indeed it is for all very old events. But there can be no shadow of doubt that he did, for the signs of that victory are all around us. Every ancient parish church has a list of vicars whose names after 1066 suddenly become Norman; many of the words we use, particularly in legal affairs, bear traces of Norman French. In the same way the most convincing evidence for the Resurrection is not so much the manuscripts themselves, though they are remarkably full, but the after-effects – the unquenchable life and vigour of the early Church. The Church may not be able to explain the Resurrection, but the Resurrection certainly explains the Church.

There are two results of the Resurrection which are worth following up at this point.

The first is the added insight it gives us into the nature of the paradoxical God we are puzzling over. He is clearly the master of death. This is, of course, implicit in what we have seen of the God of History and Creation; but the Resurrection underlines it. That great horizon of life, beyond which we cannot see, frightens us, but not him. For God does not look at it from our point of view. He can see the scenery beyond, and knows that at death we do not drop off the edge of life into a dark void, but continue our journey through a different landscape.

It is also comforting to know that this great God values us as people. If he loves us now as the individuals we are, it seems that he is determined that after death we shall remain *us*, with our personalities and relationships preserved. This, of course, may be heaven or hell – it depends on what our personalities and relationships are like. The resurrected body of Jesus, identifiable, known by others, and knowing others, shows that God loves people, and wishes us to survive as people. There is no room in Christianity for the idea that there is some great sea of heavenly divinity into which we drop and are lost forever; the Resurrection is a resurrection of personality, for only people can love, and God is Love.

The second point is that the Resurrection is not just an academic study in ancient phenomena, but a living experience proved in the lives of ordinary Christian people.

There are habitual criminals in prison, so alienated from the community and any real relationships that in terms of being social human beings they could have been declared dead. Yet Christ has so appeared to them and resurrected them that the old spiral of misery has been broken and they have been lifted to a completely different level of life, and have begun to live again.

There are gunmen in Northern Ireland who have been dead to compassion, understanding, and ordinary humanity, but who have been touched by Christ and now spend their lives trying to heal their wounded community – their death has been turned to life.

On a less dramatic scale many Christian men and women could tell of their times of suffering and sorrow, when instead of being devastated, they have found an inner life and power that has both surprised them and supported them. If we live with Jesus, and if necessary suffer and die with him, we shall rise with him too.

The Christian may argue about what actually happened on that first Easter Sunday, and may get as confused as anyone else about what happened and how. But the one thing there is never any disagreement about is the spiritual *fact* of the Resurrection. To feel the finger of God causing a resurrection in one's own life needs no other evidence and no other argument – it speaks for itself.

10 *The Offensive Weapon*

It happened in a little village church in Cleveland a few months ago when, in the course of the morning service, the minister preached on 'the armour of God'.

The historical background was familiar. The letter this word picture came from was written by St Paul while he was arrested and chained by the wrist to a Roman soldier. Day and night the soldier was there to prevent him escaping. If we feel sorry for St Paul, we cannot help having some twinge of sympathy too for the soldier, whoever he was. Paul described himself at the time as 'an envoy in chains', which he literally was. While restricted in this way he wrote to the Christians in Ephesus, that great port and metropolis of the eastern Mediterranean. He tried to find an illustration to encourage his readers to continue their mission regardless of the difficulties and enmity surrounding them. 'Of course!' he must have cried. 'Here I am, chained to the perfect example!' So Paul looked up at the soldier and found a Christian parallel for each item of his kit.

First there was the belt which every soldier wore; his sword hung from it, and it enabled him to move quickly without getting tangled up in his clothing. 'Take the belt of truth,' Paul urged. Then he looked at the soldier's breastplate, designed to protect him against any fatal blow – 'Take the breastplate of uprightness and integrity,' he added. Then he looked down at the soldier's sandals, the footwear that gave the Roman army their reputation for relentless movement – 'Take the good news of peace on your feet.'

Then Paul thought of the great battle shield which the soldier used in the heaviest fighting; perhaps it was propped up in the corner. It was the defence against one of the nastiest weapons of those days, the arrow tipped with tow, dipped in pitch and lit. The great oblong battle shield was a clever laminate of two kinds of wood glued together, the softer sort on the outside. When a burning arrow hit it, the tip sank into the soft wood and went out, while the hard wood behind stopped the head from penetrating – 'Take the shield of faith,' Paul wrote.

Then, possibly lying on the table, there would have been the soldier's helmet, made of metal and leather to protect his head – 'Take the helmet of salvation,' continued Paul. Then he looked at the sword, the short Roman sword used in close action fighting – 'Take the sword of the Spirit, which is the word of God.'

At this point I came to a full stop, my mind switched to a different track, and I went off on my own private journey of exploration. What did St Paul mean by that last parallel – 'the sword of the Spirit which is the word of God?'

One thing becomes obvious – of the items Paul mentions, the sword is the only offensive weapon; all the others are defensive items designed to protect the combatant. The sword is different; it is the Christian's only weapon of *attack*, and is therefore very important. It is 'the word of God'; but what did he mean by that? 'The Word of God' is a well used title used to describe the Bible, but Paul could not have meant that, because the Old Testament hadn't been put together by that date, and none of the New Testament had been written at all. Could he have meant what St John wrote in his Gospel – the *logos* of God? Again no, because this was a good twenty years before St John made the connection between the *logos* and Jesus.

It was in this state of puzzlement that I spent the rest of

what I assume was an excellent sermon, determined to get to the bottom of the matter as soon as I got home. It turned out that the difficulty lay in the English translation; there is much more meaning in the Greek which Paul wrote than can be shown in English. The word Paul used means a total speech, an entire proclamation. So a more accurate translation would be, 'Your sword, your only offensive weapon, is the proclamation of the Gospel which the Spirit will give you.'

The message of this is that the most powerful weapon in a Christian's armoury is the proclamation of his faith; it has a cutting edge which gets through the protective prejudice of the enemy's mind, and a stabbing point which reaches the heart. But it also means that these words are given to us at the time we need them, by the Holy Spirit; the sword is handed to us in the heat of battle.

It is this mention of a Holy Spirit that puzzles Christians and non-Christians alike - Just what, or who, is it?

In trying to answer this question we are again forced back to an agnostic position of saying that in the end we don't know, for we are dealing with the mysterious nature of a paradoxical God.

The story of the early Christians, and of Christians ever since, has not been of thinking up a doctrine and then looking for an experience to fit it, but the other way round - of saying, 'God, what's happening to me?' After the religious realities have been found, and the spiritual phenomena have been experienced, then comes the problem of how to fit them in to some kind of sensible pattern. This is what makes theology so interesting, because it is the study of a moving target, an active God. It also explains why it is so much easier to pin down what God did in the past, than what he is doing now, or going to do in the future.

The experience the early disciples had on that first Whitsunday, of flickering flames and mighty winds, and an infusion of power unknown before, left them bewildered and stunned, and they were hard put to find words for it. Jesus had spoken to them in cryptic terms of a 'comforter' and a 'spirit of truth'; so they called it, or him, the Holy Spirit, or Holy Ghost, because they had to find a name of some sort. The experience was real enough; it was the placing of it in the right context which was difficult.

This confusion has continued down the centuries, for Christian thinking about the Holy Spirit has always been vague and controversial. As Kenneth Greet put it: if when reaching home we said, 'I met so-and-so's father in the street,' everyone would feel normal because the word 'father' is familiar. If when we got home we said 'I met a spirit,' or 'a ghost', the response would be rather different. The term has a spookiness about it which doesn't help.

Another reason for puzzlement is that the ebb and flow of argument about the Holy Spirit down the centuries has become so complex and convoluted that it makes the ordinary mind despair.

A further reason is the very materialism of the modern world, which is so different from the more psychologically open world in which the New Testament was written. Anything with the word 'spirit' in it causes a revulsion in the modern mind, and lumps those who believe in it with people who believe in fairies.

The Church, after centuries of argument, eventually reached the conclusion that God was a combination of God the Father, God the Son, and God the Holy Spirit – three persons, yet one at the same time. In other words, they concluded that God touched them from three different directions, and in three different ways, but they couldn't explain how; the truth was a paradox.

This formula, however, can only be a totally inadequate form of words to impose a pattern on a welter of divine experiences. Fortunately it is the experience, not the formula, which is important.

So what are these experiences? They are fragmentary like a picture in a child's kaleidoscope, brilliant patterns in a symmetrical design one moment, and then another pattern with different colours predominating. The challenge is to find a meaning in each fragment of brilliant colour, in each pattern, and behind the changing of the patterns. Over the years some common and constant insights have been found to tell us something about the Holy Spirit.

The first significant point is that the first disciples used the word *pneuma*; it is the Greek word for 'spirit' and also means 'wind' (as in 'pneumatic'). They got this idea from the Jewish religion (for they were Jews), where the Hebrew word for the spirit of God, *ruach*, also meant 'wind'. The *ruach* was the overwhelming wind of the desert, the elemental force, incalculable, irresistible and invisible, and it not only shaped the sand-dunes but also man's behaviour. It was this *ruach* which the Jews thought of as the breath of God; a superhuman energy which filled the prophets' mouths with words, and the warriors' hearts with courage. When God knelt down and made the first man and woman, like a child playing with modelling clay, they visualized him breathing into these passive models the *ruach* to make them living souls.

So on that first Whitsunday, when the disciples met and experienced what they called 'the rushing of a violent wind', their experience of the Holy Spirit fitted with their Jewish background; it was experience of sheer, brute power.

Another element they found was an added and enhanced comradeship, a deepened fellowship with each other and with God. They spoke of the Holy Spirit as if he were just another, but very dominant member of their group whose decision was final. 'It seemed good to the Holy Spirit and to us', was the kind of thing they often said. The Book of Acts has quite rightly been called 'The Acts of the Holy Spirit', for this unseen presence seems to have dictated all the movements and thought up all the initiatives, some of them quite hair-raising.

For example, the Holy Spirit tells Philip to do something stupid, to go out and wait by the main road, when there must have been so much more work to be done back home. He tells Peter to do something illegal in Jewish law, to actually visit a Roman centurion in his home; and he had to tell him several times until he went. He tells a poor inoffensive Christian in Damascus who was trying not to be noticed, to virtually commit suicide by going to the main persecutor and telling him who he was.

These, and many other stories of amazing adventures and divine coincidences, would be told from Christian to Christian, and handed down to those who followed them; and as they were passed on, so each group would add their own examples from their experience. They felt that the Holy Spirit was their great unseen strength, preparing the way they should go, and helping them to do and say the right thing when they got there.

Modern Christians can not only testify that these kinds of things still happen, but would also give credit to the Holy Spirit for the very survival of the Christian community itself.

It has been truly said that every large organization has within it the seeds of its own decay. Be it an empire, a nation, a multi-national company, a financial conglomerate, it will build on small beginnings, grow, harden and solidify, and as if eaten from within by a social canker, eventually drop apart. If the Church were just a human organization there is no reason why it should not be subject to this cycle of social life and death. Indeed, in many senses it is, for it is a very human organization. Looking back over the centuries, we can see the times when the Church has almost died on its feet. Every two or three hundred years the fire seems to have died down, and the structure started to crumble: third-century heresies, the Dark Ages, medieval corruption, eighteenth-century carelessness, at each point there were people bewailing the death of the Church.

Yet the Church seems to have within it not only the seeds of its own decay, but also the seeds of its own renewal, and from the crumbling ruins of the old Church has sprung each time a new vital growth, vibrant with life and new vision. Many would say that this is the work of the Holy Spirit.

To change the picture, every few hundred years, when the Church's edge becomes blunt, the Holy Spirit takes it, plunges it into the fire, and hammers it on the anvil of the world until the rust and dross have gone and it is bright and sharp again.

The essence of the action of the Holy Spirit is power and movement, which is why the word 'wind' is so suitable. We cannot tell where the wind has come from or where it is going; it can be a whispering zephyr or a howling gale; it can cool and comfort, or sweep us off our feet and blow our houses down; we cannot see it, but the effects of its movements are obvious – and yet if we bottle some to examine it, it has gone! The 'Holy Wind' is a fine picture, for it matches the Christian experience.

But how is it possible for Christians to achieve a quality of life that was impossible before they followed Christ – as they so often seem to do? Paul saw that there was more involved than human dedication and will-power. There was a divine dynamic; it was the only reasonable answer. The Holy Spirit gives gifts, and causes fruits of his indwelling power to grow in the heart.

First, Paul thinks of the gifts that are given to every Christian. In a letter to Corinth, he says that there are three main gifts: faith, hope, and above all, love. In his letter to the people in Galatia he mentions the fruits of the Spirit: love, joy, peace, patience, kindness, goodness, faithfulness, gentleness and self-control.

But then Paul goes on to say that there are gifts of the Holy Spirit which are given to some and not to others: like speaking in public, healing, prophecy, speaking in tongues. No one gift is better, or commands more prestige, than any other; they are gifts held in trust.

The students at Balliol College in the 1870s wrote a play in which appeared the rhyme

> My name is George Nathaniel Curzon,
> I am a most superior person.

How offensive we find someone who arrogantly assumes that he is better than anyone else; and how much more sympathetic we find someone who acknowledges modestly that his gifts are given by God. The Christian should see that every gift comes with a work-sheet attached; the gift must not be left unused, nor used selfishly. Whatever gift the Holy Spirit has given us must be developed, trained and used for others.

A rather silly story underlines the point. A man dreamed that he was in heaven, window-shopping along the main street. He was attracted by a fruiterers called Gabriel Bros Ltd, for in the window was a sign saying, 'Fruits of the Spirit sold here'. Entering the shop he was greeted by an angel who smiled at him and said, 'Good morning sir, take a seat sir, what can I get you sir?'

This confirmed his impression that he was in heaven! 'Well,' he said, 'I want some fruits of the Spirit. I'll have some joy for the wife – she's been a bit of a misery these days; and some love for the children – they just regard me as a walking wallet; and some patience for my boss – he's been a bit tetchy recently; and some long-suffering for myself.'

'Certainly,' said the angel, who then went to the cupboards

behind the counter. Soon he laid down by the till several little brown paper envelopes. 'Here we are, sir. A packet of joy, and one each of love, patience and long-suffering. Take them with our compliments.'

The man looked at the little packets with some dismay; they were not at all what he expected.

'Ah,' said the angel. 'I know that expression, so perhaps I ought to explain. Though the sign in the window says "Fruits of the Spirit", nobody actually sells them - well, we couldn't, could we! We only sell the seeds - you have to grow them yourself!'

11 *The Church Idiotic*

Groucho Marx made certain of his place in history by declaring that he certainly wouldn't join any club that would have *him* as a member. The Church, militant, triumphant, and on many occasions idiotic, makes the same statement, for it is the only organization designed to accommodate all the people who are by nature unqualified to join it. Even worse, if they found anyone who thought that he *was* qualified to join it, they ought to throw him out!

It follows that the Church is the natural home for the inadequate, the weak, and the downright odd, as well as some ordinary people. Sometimes, when beset by 100-page letters written in multi-coloured ball point, sitting through committees of mind-numbing irrelevance, or being woken up at 3 a.m. by lonely people just wanting a chat, I am tempted to look at the ceiling and say, wearily, 'Lord, why are your best friends such out-and-out idiots?' A friend once said to me, 'The Church doesn't get much fruit these days, but boy, we've got the nuts!'

Fortunately for most of us, our oddness or a high score on the 'nuttiness-scale' doesn't debar us from playing our full part in Jesus' Church – cynics might even think that it helps! An archdeacon once confided to me that he thought the Almighty allowed the Church to survive to preserve a sense of humour among the angels.

But what *is* the Church? In order to tease out its true nature we first have to dispose of the most common misconceptions, what it most definitely is NOT.

It is not a social club for the elderly who like a nice quiet sit once or twice a week, and where they can relieve their loneliness by meeting other people.

It is not a society for the preservation of medieval or mid-Victorian buildings by a frantic round of jumble sales, garden parties, or if fair means fail, Christmas bazaars.

Neither is it a music appreciation society of buffs who prefer Bach to heavy metal, interspersed with soothing talks to take the stress and strain out of life.

It is not even, and this might be nearer the bone, a club for conserving the essence of Englishness, a sort of cultural society to reverence our roots, our past heroes, and promote the best of our civilized standards.

Thoroughly worthy as all these activities may be, and beneficially as many Christians may get involved in them, they are not the core of what the Church of Jesus actually is. When you think about it, the nature of the Church boils down to one very simple ingredient. *Simple*, it should be emphasized, not *easy*.

The Church is the company of people who have felt the touch of Jesus on their lives and have decided to follow him. Whether that touch has been a full-blown dramatic appearance of the Risen Christ saying 'Follow me', as was the case with Paul and many others since; or whether it was a quiet and steady progression to the point where that influence built up to an irresistible inner compulsion – that touch of 'otherness' must be real, and our willingness to follow must be sincere.

Naturally, that first experience is only the start; we are, at this stage, just new recruits as Peter, James, John and the rest were in their time. All we know is that we have heard him say 'Follow me', have seen the look in his eyes, and are following. We realize that we do not know where it is going to lead, God help us! For Jesus goes into some very dangerous places, and we are expected to follow one step at a time without knowing the destination. We also know that this means making his work ours, taking up his ministry, and perhaps, even having to carry a cross.

It was the simple statement of Peter, 'You are the son of God', that was, and is, the basis of the Christian community; not acceptance of vast formulas of doctrine, or even evidence of decent moral behaviour, but a recognition of Jesus as the human face of a paradoxical God, and a willingness to follow at whatever cost.

The Church is always within one, or at the most two, generations of extinction. Were it not for a continuous stream of people who feel that touch and respond individually and personally, the Church would die very quickly indeed. It is this one-to-one commitment which is the rock on which the vast structure of the Christian Church, holy, catholic, and apostolic, is built.

An addition to this, which is not so much a rule as a sign of goodwill, is that we should expect to continue, in answer to Jesus' simple request to his followers, to pass round the bread and wine, and remember him. Call it the Mass, Eucharist, Holy Communion, or Breaking of Bread, it is basically the continuing of a custom that he asked them to do as a personal favour to him, and it seems churlish to refuse. It is, in fact, an acting out of the scene in the Upper Room at the Last Supper. The priest or minister takes the part of Jesus, and the congregation take the part of the twelve disciples, and Jesus is remembered.

It is not, however, just a static, dead act of remembrance, for Jesus said that when even two or three of his followers are gathered together he would be in the middle of them. Where better can that happen than in the little ceremony of remembrance which he began? Let theologians argue, if it amuses them, as to *where* he is, in the bread, in the wine, or wherever; it matters little so long as the presence of their Lord is in the hearts of his people.

There are some groups of Christians, like the Salvation Army, who have severe doubts about this simple practice, and do not observe it because of the disagreements it can cause. This is a sad commentary on the fear and foolishness of Christian people down the centuries who have been so afraid that the purity of this profound little ceremony might be watered down that they have surrounded it with great superstructures of rituals and words. Human nature being what it is, and the Church being by no means short of that quality, what one would expect to happen, does. People define, argue, disagree and split apart, deadly things like spiritual pride creep in, until Christians make it much more difficult to attend their re-creation of the Last Supper than Jesus did at the original one. So what was designed as a focus for unity among his followers becomes a scandalous symbol of their disunity, and a monument to the folly of Christians ever imagining that they can out-think God.

In spite of this, the sharing of the bread and wine is still a symbol of the unity of Christians all over the world. There are people in lonely prison cells, remote jungle villages, and in vast imposing cathedrals, all sharing the bread and wine. They dress it up in various rituals, from a simple *ad hoc* meal to a complicated and very long extravaganza of music, colour and light. They speak in thousands of languages that we do not understand, and sing in styles we could not hope to follow. Yet all are doing basically the same thing, and if any Christian were suddenly transported into their company, as soon as they started to share the bread and wine he would feel at home.

This does not only apply all round the world, but also down the centuries. As we have seen, every few hundred years the Church has hardened into a chrysalis and then broken out into a new and different looking appearance. Suppose that we could take a time machine and use it to go back to the early Church in Rome who met, amid persecution, in the underground cemeteries, or to the deserts where the early monks and hermits lived, or to join the wandering Celtic saints with their peculiar hair-cuts, or to spy on the overpowering symbolism of the medieval Church. In every case we should find ourselves in situations and practices that would be very strange to us – until the moment when the bread and the wine was shared; then we would realize where we were and whom we were among.

For Christianity is a team game; we have to be one of a group, part of a fellowship. A Christian can be an individualist but never an isolationist. If I told someone, 'I'm a footballer,' his immediate response would be, 'Oh, which team do you play for?' If I answered that I didn't play for a team, I played football by myself, he would alter the question to 'What mental hospital do you come from?' Just in this way, if we tell someone that we are Christians, the perfectly proper question is, 'What church do you attend?'

In a sense, of all the world religions Christianity is the least spiritual and the most materialistic. There is little space for disembodied spirits flying around, spiritual feelings that have no practical results, or great seas of formless infinity. From the crying baby in the dirty cradle at Bethlehem, to the strange but real body of the resurrected Jesus, there is a down-to-earth objectivity about it all. So to talk of a spiritual relationship to God without a real relationship to fellow-believers seems out of character to a Christian.

Some people talk about an 'invisible Church' comprised of those people who are following Jesus but who won't join any organised church. While having every sympathy with those who look at the Church Idiotic and decide that it is not for them, it is difficult to see how they can survive without the practical step of saying to a fellow-Christian, 'Hello, can I help?'

Of course, the Church must have the modesty to admit that God's membership lists may not match very well with those in the vicar's filing cabinet. Many of those who sing 'Lord, Lord,' most loudly in S, A, T or B, may not be 'in' after all; but it is still difficult to see how an isolated Christian can do without the stimulus, encouragement and challenge of the rest. You have only to take a single piece of coal from a roaring fire, place it on the hearth, and watch it go out by itself, to see the point.

Another aspect is that, if the Church has something of God about it, it is not only a human institution, but in some way bridges the barrier of death. If those who live and die with Jesus are raised with him, then the fellowship of the Church must be continued in some form beyond the grave. It is a homely thought that, when we get beyond the Church Militant here on earth, we are 'promoted to glory' as the Salvation Army say, and join the Church Triumphant in heaven.

The Christian is convinced that fellowship with other followers of Jesus here and now can only be enhanced, and not destroyed, by death. The number of Christians living now are only a small proportion of those who have lived before, and it can be no hardship to be invited to join the majority.

A soldier in the First World War passed a small village church in France as the service ended. The priest was shaking hands with the handful of people who had attended the service. 'Not many at church this morning, Father,' he said sarcastically. 'That's where you're wrong,' retorted the priest, waving his hands in the air. 'There were millions and millions!'

All in all, the fact that there is a Church, fallible and faulty as it is, can only be good news to Christians, who would be lost without it. As the sentence in the creed, 'I believe in the holy and universal Church' makes clear, the Church is not just an organization for promoting the good news of Jesus; it is part of the good news itself.

Looking at the Bible to see what it says of the Church, we find, as usual, a gallery of word-pictures, each sketch making its own point.

The first picture is one that appealed to many hymn writers: it is of a great temple for God – a building in which his will is done. 'The Church's one foundation is Jesus Christ her Lord', 'Christ is our corner-stone, on him alone we build' are typical. Every Christian is a brick in this holy structure, each generation contributes something to it, and the opening ceremony will be accompanied by the final trumpets at the end of time. Think of what an ancient cathedral is like. Down among the foundations there may be a Saxon crypt, above some doorways there may be Norman arches, various parts of it may be Early English, Perpendicular, and Gothic; there may be some Elizabethan or Jacobean woodwork, a twentieth-century tapestry, and almost certainly a Victorian heating system that is too expensive to run. It is a hotch-potch of styles and techniques, but it also has an impressive unity of purpose about it.

So the picture of the Church as the Temple of God makes the point that every Christian has a vital part to play, has an appointed place in the plan, and that the overall aim is to construct an edifice worthy of God.

A second picture is of the Church as the Bride of Christ. There is nothing like a wedding to prove that happiness is infectious. People thoroughly enjoy seeing a young couple dewy-eyed and nervous, delightfully in love with each other. Bystanders will crowd round waiting for them to come out of the church porch. The bridegroom doesn't worry about how well she can cook, or make her own clothes. She doesn't worry about whether he has good prospects in his job, or can mend the fuses when they blow. Not then, not at the wedding. Those concerns come afterwards. For the moment all that matters is that they love each other, and they know that this love is returned - and so they make their vows to each other.

The picture Paul drew is of the Church not only as the *wife* of Christ, but as his *bride.* Christ loves his followers like a bridegroom loves his bride. He loves his Church with all its faults, fears and fantasies, with all its blindness and half-heartedness. In spite of all that, they are his people, they have exchanged their vows, they are surrounded by his love and, most of the time at least, they love him back.

A third picture is of the Church as Christ's body. This has become so much part of the language that the very term 'church members' comes from it, ' 'member' being an arm or a leg. Christ is no longer on this earth in a material way, except through his followers. Therefore if he wants a job done he has to get one of his people to do it. If he wants a child taught, an invalid healed or a starving person fed, he has to find someone to do it; if he wants a story told or a sermon preached, he has to find a voice to speak for him.

There are several aspects of this picture that stick in the Christian mind, but the obvious one is obedience. Our bodies are, after all, only a convenient way of carrying our heads around and of doing what our heads require to be done. As the head of the Body of the Church is Christ, clearly we must do what the head says. If we do not function at all we turn Christ into a paralytic, whereas if we act on our own initiative without reference to the head, we turn him into a spastic. The Church exists to do what Christ wants, no more, and no less. Sometimes he may ask his body to do what seems pointless, painful or puerile; but if the Church is his hands and feet, his voice and his compassionate embrace, then the Church must sigh and buckle down to doing it.

These three main pictures, and several others we haven't mentioned, have the authority of the Bible, but they are only pictures, illustrations to make a point. However, there is one moral they all have – an emphasis on the unity that Christians ought to have between themselves. Without that unity the Temple becomes a heap of rubble, the Bride becomes a schizophrenic, and the Body of Christ falls apart.

This is why there is so much concern about Church unity today, not because of whatever practical benefits it would bring, but because disunity is a denial of the Christian's basic understanding of the Church. Although, mercifully, the antagonisms between Christians are very small compared with the splits in other world religions, and although unity does not mean uniformity, nevertheless Christians should not rest until there is an overall unity of regard, respect and purpose among all the members of the Church. But what kind of unity will this be, and how can it be found?

Church unity cannot mean that everyone has to understand God in exactly the same way. As we have seen, to try to reduce the paradoxical God to human sense and language is an impossibility anyway, so no one could, or should, dare to say that their understanding is right and everyone else's is wrong. For our comprehension of God is a developing thing individual to us. It is made up of fragments of the Sunday School lessons we may have heard, the books we have read, the people we have met, all fired together in the experience of life that we have. The Bible has influenced us, so has the historical teaching of the Church and its creeds. Add to this our own 'inner light', as the Quakers call it, and we each have our own distinctive and individual understanding of God and the world.

Naturally, this private 'cosmic view' continually develops, changes and refines as our experience and knowledge grows. Long may it do so, for the biggest danger is to aim at being consistent. For one side of our understanding often grows faster than another. Inconsistency is a sign of growth, for the only time anything can be totally consistent is when it is dead. Long may the ideas in our heads clash against each other, insights contradict, and understandings deepen.

There are always five gospels: Matthew, Mark, Luke, John and yours.

So although a Christian's understanding is almost bound to fall broadly into the rough shape of the classic formulas that the Church has found to be proved by the acid test of time, there is still plenty of space for each Christian to come to his own conclusions. The Christian can think and let think, for his unity with other Christians does not lie in a common understanding of what a Christian believes.

Neither does it lie in a common culture. One does not need to be involved with a particular denomination long to realize that it has its own tradition, ethos, and atmosphere. Another BBC religious producer and I once spent a happy teatime describing them all – gastronomically. We came to the conclusion that the Church of England was a cucumber sandwich, the Roman Catholics a pint of stout, the Methodists fish and chips, and the Salvation Army a hot-dog with plenty of onions and mustard. The Quakers, we decided, would be fasting! Each church has its own taste, its own history, mores, and culture.

This culture is not only a very good thing, but a thoroughly Christian thing, for it is the working out in earthly terms of a spiritual fellowship. The Church of England, for example, tries to cope with the spiritual needs of the people from the christening at the church porch to the burial in 'God's acre'. By weekly worship, pastoral care, and family contact it tries to foster the growth of living in this world by the standards of the next. It provides a spiritual home where casualties can find first aid, the happy can share their joy, and the lonely be surrounded by love and care. This, at its best, is what the Church does. However, in the Church of England's case, *how* it does it is coloured by a whole catalogue of historical accidents, from Henry VIII's divorce, Cranmer's prose and Queen Elizabeth's compromise, onwards. The fact that the priest is called a vicar or rector, that there is a bishop, that candles are on the altar, and that psalms are chanted, are all historical accidents that have become part of the church culture that Anglicans value.

This culture is good – at its best it is magnificent – but then the same could be said for the Roman Catholic culture, the Presbyterian culture, the Methodist culture, and all the others. They all fill for their own people the same spiritual and pastoral needs, but the historical accidents in their cases are different. So some will have bishops, some will not; some will use candles, some will not; some will chant psalms, some sing them, and some will not use them at all. The job is the same, but the ways of doing it, the style, the language, the forms of structure are all very different.

Fortunately, or unfortunately, there is no way of wiping out the effects of history, or ignoring the differences in church cultures to which people hold so tenaciously. All we can do is be thankful that to belong to a church culture is good both for us and for others, and to recognize that church unity does not depend on a uniformity of culture and tradition.

Where then can we find this holy grail, the identity card the Church lost soon after it was issued? Surely, the only thing that holds the Christian family together is a common faith in Jesus as the Christ – that will always be the rock on which the Church is built. That is the one common denominator every Christian has, whichever tradition he may belong to. It is this central love and loyalty to Jesus that holds Christians together in spite of differing views and varied backgrounds; this shared faith should, and usually does, overcome all other differences.

Methodists are very fond of quoting John Wesley's conversion experience in Aldersgate Street, when after listening to a reading of Luther's preface to the Epistle to the Romans he said, 'I felt my heart strangely warmed . . .' But the point lies in the rest of what he said, '. . . because I felt I did trust in Christ, Christ alone.' It is that trust, that faith which is not only the bedrock of everything the Church stands for, but also the only possible and legitimate foundation for its unity.

When two people have that basic relationship with Jesus they can brush aside all the traditional barriers, all the ancient and modern stupidities of the Church Idiotic, and laugh as, in fellowship, they shake each other's hand.

12 *A Sense of the Ridiculous*

It may seem irrelevant, but the one word that keeps coming to mind when the subject of prayer, public or private is mentioned, is the word 'ridiculous'.

Think of the attitudes various groups of people have evolved for this activity. Some people kneel down and touch the ground with their foreheads like the ancient Jews (this is what the Bible means when it says 'they fell on their faces before him'). Others believe that absolute isolation is necessary, like Simeon Stylites who spent thirty-five years on top of a pillar, but who had to build it higher and higher to avoid the crowds who came to watch. (It never seemed to occur to him that the higher he built the more people would come to see him.) Some people pray by rocking backwards and forwards, some stand with their hands in the air, some pray all together out loud in languages no one can understand, some kneel, and some adopt the position known as 'the non-conformist crouch' which is guaranteed to give both indigestion *and* backache. To an unprepared observer it might seem that the conditions for prayer are that it should feel uncomfortable and undignified, and that it should look ridiculous.

Then consider the reasons for prayer. Could there be anything more silly than trying to draw God's attention to something? We rightly laugh at the story about the minister who is supposed to have prayed, 'Lord, as you have no doubt seen on page six of today's Guardian . . .' After all, if God is not more acutely aware of what is going on than we are, he would certainly not be worth worshipping. If the New Testament is right, and God knows us better than we know ourselves, and knows our words before we have thought of uttering them, there seems something inherently pointless about saying anything to him at all. Not only that, but if he not only knows *more*, but knows *better* than we do, then our prayers will probably be wrong and unfulfillable anyway. Cannot we rely on him to do his best for us without special pleading? If we feel that we have to badger him with requests, that could be called doubt, not faith – doubt in a good and all-providing God.

In any case, what is God to do if one devout farmer asks for steady rain to water his lettuces, while on the other side of the hedge an equally pious farmer prays for sunshine to ripen the hay?

Looked at logically, prayer is absurd.

When Jesus talked about prayer, he too gave free rein to his sense of the ridiculous, but the other way round. He said that God was like a father who wouldn't give his child a clip round the ear when he asks for a packet of crisps. He is like a friend whom you knock up at midnight to borrow some bread, and who tells you in unmistakable words to visit a taxidermist, but you keep knocking and in the end he throws a loaf at you – hard! Or God is like a 'bent' magistrate who won't hear the case of a poor widow because she can't bribe him, but because he can't go in and out of his house without tripping over the insistent old lady, he eventually gives in.

All these stories seem to have a touch of the ridiculous about them because, one has to assume, Jesus felt that it was ridiculous to have to defend prayer at all.

So what is prayer all about? As the little girl said to her father when she first saw an elephant at the zoo, 'Daddy, what's it *for*?'

The heart of it must be the building of a relationship

between us and that great paradoxical God our minds cannot comprehend. We have pictured him living on a great sea of mystery beyond the shores of our understanding. Yet the tides of this sea wash in and out of our lives, splashing our conscious and sub-conscious minds. God is not far away, but closer than is often comfortable. Prayer is not the art of using the right words, or indeed any words at all, but of being on his wavelength and aware of him.

The most entertaining television and radio programmes come into every home, but we do not get the benefit of any of them unless our receiving sets are properly tuned to pick them up. As Mother Teresa has said, 'Prayer enlarges the heart until it is capable of containing God's gift of himself.'

Prayer, when we boil it all down, is just a two-way conversation with God. Like a child with its father, the talk doesn't need to be an agonizing confrontation, except on the rare occasions when we have been especially bad. Most of the time he is just as happy to hear us chatter about our equivalent of marbles, conkers, or school, to tell us a story, or if for much of the time we just sit on his lap and say nothing at all!

One of the great contemplative monks, Brother Lawrence, was such a simple yet holy man that when he died in 1691 a few of his letters and conversations were gathered together in a book called *The Practice of the Presence of God.* In it he tells how he felt the presence of God just as much, if not more, surrounded by the clatter and bustle of the kitchen where he was the monastery cook, than he did in the solemnity of the chapel. 'I have quitted all forms of devotion and set prayers save those which my state obliges me. And I take it my only business to persevere in his holy presence by simple attention . . . to a silent and secret, constant intercourse of the soul with God.'

The comic adventures of Don Camillo should be on every

Christian's bookshelf. This lovable but ham-fisted country priest regularly pops into his church to have a chat with the Christ on his crucifix. Their conversations, profound, wide-ranging and often funny, seem to sum up much of what prayer is all about.

For prayer is not words, but the closeness of a relationship; it is not a technique, but an awareness of someone else. Ole Halesby put it well when he described it as 'nothing more involved than lying in the sunshine of God's grace'.

The concept of prayer is as beautiful as that of faith, for neither depends on intellect, reputation, or even talent. The simple, ignorant, naïve person can get as near to God in prayer as anyone else, and probably quicker, for the self-sufficient do not pray, the self-satisfied don't want to, and the self-righteous can't.

Most ordinary people pray, though they don't know they are doing it and wouldn't use the word. Every time we stay silent before a breathtaking view, every time we are rocked back on our heels by the picture of a starving child in Africa, or cannot say anything to a person whose pain communicates with us; in those brief moments when words fail we seem to be in touch with something outside ourselves, or deep inside ourselves. We are told that explorers who set out to cross vast open spaces, single-handed sailors who launch out into the great oceans, also find this happening to them. We could explain this in religious language and say that at those times when we have put out a finger and touched the paradox at the heart of life – the paradox where God lives – we have prayed.

So with prayer the vital thing is the relationship built up with God. This is the melody, everything else is harmony; and without it nothing will or can happen. Which leads us to the subject of prayers which ask for things.

If we ask for something we want to *be*, for instance to be generous enough to forgive someone who has done a dirty trick on us at work, or to forgive a difficult neighbour, the answer is usually 'Yes'. For this quality can only help the world God wants; our act of prayer has cleared the path to our door, and so God is able to deliver the power to forgive.

But if we ask for something we want to *have*, perhaps success in an application for a job, that can be much more difficult. Taking such a loving interest in us as he does, God has a pretty good idea of where he wants us to be, and his ideas might not be at all the same as ours; so he sometimes slams doors in our faces. Also we might not be ready for that job *yet*; we might have more to learn, perhaps about life, about people, and about ourselves, before we are qualified from God's point of view. When we ask for *things* we have to appreciate that we can only see our own interests. God sees other people's as well, and his own. Frustrating and demoralizing as it is, our prayer always has to end with the sentiment, 'In spite of what I want, God, may your will, not mine, be done.'

This is not to say that praying for things is wrong, or that this kind of prayer is never answered, for an encyclopaedia could be filled with quite incredible answers to prayer, and every good Christian community could compile its own. But we have to remember that the basic relationship has to be there, the door to our lives must be open; and that the answer may be 'No' or 'Not yet'.

One thing is certain, and borne out by experience, that it is possible for God to answer our prayers. If there is enough space and flexibility for man to manipulate nature as we do, there is no reason to doubt that God can do better. The secret is knowledge, for as mankind gets to know how all the natural laws work, so we can use them and adapt them for our purposes. As God made the world and designed it he is, presumably, all past, present, and future Nobel Prize winners rolled into one. To know all about the natural laws is to have them plastic in his hands. God's power to answer prayer is not in question – his willingness is. The words, 'Not as we in our ignorance would wish, but as you in your wisdom know best', are acted on by God, whether we say them or not.

Moving away from private prayer to public prayer and praise we are on a related subject, and another aspect of the ridiculous.

There seems to be no physical contortion, or public exhibition known to man, that has not been used by someone, somewhere to express Christian worship. The 'Shakers' danced around in slow circles, the medieval Church used blazes of colour and clouds of incense, Puritans used stupefyingly long sermons, enthusiastic groups stay up all night praying themselves to fever pitch, and monks get up in the middle of the night to say a choral 'good morning' to God.

And for what? In order to supply the Almighty with a continuous world-wide diet of flattery? Is he the kind of God who needs surrounding by a vast concourse of obsequious yes-men? On the face of it, public worship in its purpose and practice often seems faintly, and occasionally seems highly, ridiculous.

In attempting to answer the question, 'What is it for, anyway?' we have to admit that worship is mostly to our advantage, not God's. It does several very useful things for our spiritual benefit.

First it reinforces our commitment. The word 'worship' comes from the Anglo-Saxon and means 'worth-ship' – ascribing to someone their true worth. So we address the mayor of our town as 'Your Worship', giving him the honour due to his worth as the first citizen in the community. When a Christian worships he gives God his worth as his primary aim and his first loyalty. Christians do not worship a code of morals, or even a catalogue of commandments, but a person.

If the classic prayers of the Christian Church are examined carefully they are, in fact, remarkably short on divine flattery. In Cranmer's wonderful prose, which is at the root of so much English worship, there is just one simple title for God, followed by the particular quality the prayer is concerned with; such as, 'Almighty God, the giver of all good gifts . . .' or, 'O God, whose nature and property is always to have mercy . . .'

The second thing worship does is to run through the whole of the Christian's experience of God in an artistic way, using whatever methods are most suitable in that community. It confirms in public the experiences the Christian has felt in his heart. A full act of worship, however simple or complicated, should include this gamut of experience, starting with awe and wonder at the mysteries of God, and continuing with repentance for our sins, the assurance of God's forgiveness through Jesus, dedication of ourselves to God, the proclamation of the teaching of Jesus, prayers and action for others, and the sending out of the Christians into the world to live out their faith.

Each service re-affirms what Christians have found and what the Church holds to be permanently true. In a real act of worship our own difficult-to-define feelings and hesitant faith can be fitted into the pattern of other people's experience, and we are stimulated and challenged to launch out further into the deeper water of the spiritual life.

As for the actual methods of covering this cosmos-wide universal brief, this is where the fun starts; for almost every Christian has a favourite and most appreciated style of worship.

Some get most help from silence, like the Quakers; others who prefer a more formal, historic style would be Anglicans; others who like colour, music, and drama might go to the Roman Catholics, the Orthodox Church, or the Salvation

Army; people who like to sing in a friendly atmosphere would be Pentecostals – and so on. Every denomination, and even churches within the same denomination, have evolved their own mix of sights, sounds, symbols, feelings and smells to try to communicate the parts of true worship.

There are, however, three general points which apply to them all. Worship is a two-way thing. On one of the towers of Bath Abbey there is a carving of Jacob's Ladder, a convention found in many older churches, sometimes with angels going up and down. It is supposed to be a symbol of the Church's worship, in which God's word comes down to us, and our response goes up the ladder to God.

Worship is statement and reaction, question and answer, thesis and antithesis. The wonder of God's presence is shown; our reaction is a sense of unworthiness and confession. God's forgiveness is proclaimed; which calls for the reply of the dedication of ourselves. The message of Jesus is taught; and this naturally leads to our action for others in prayer and practicalities. It is like a pendulum swinging, or the rhythm of breathing in and out. Whether the response is in hymns and choruses, sentences in an order of service, shouts of 'hallelujah!' or sensitive silences, is entirely a matter of personal taste; so long as the opportunity for response is there.

Another thing in common is the resort to ritual. Every church uses ritual, for human beings are pattern-making animals, and prefer to know where they are. Whether it is a quiet service of meditation, a sandwich of hymns, Bible reading and prayers, or a service out of a book; hide-bound or flexible, ritual it is. We ought to distinguish, however, between *ritual*, which is an inevitable and basic pattern of worship and provides a structure for the worshippers, and *ritualism* which is just the outward form without any spiritual content, and which nobody would defend.

And lastly, we need to remember that worship is trying, however imperfectly, to give expression to the mysteries of life; endeavouring to pull together the insights and faith of the whole Church. St Paul once said, 'We are stewards of the mysteries of God.' To be a trustee, steward, or churchwarden responsible for the church roof or the central heating provides headaches enough, as the people who have to do it will testify. To be charged with the job of administering the services and making sure everything goes as it should, is even more demanding. But what are we to do about being made responsible for the 'mysteries of God'?

These profound paradoxes of God's nature, his world, and his relationship to us are, as we have seen, beyond logic and language. But they are real, and can be appreciated and expressed, if not understood. Just as we may not completely understand our husbands or wives, but this certainly does not lessen the love we have for them or the value we place upon them, so the Church's task is to find ways, using every artistic method that is suitable, to illustrate the truths we can see about the God we know. Music, poetry, drama, dance, symbols, eloquent speech, ancient ceremonies, modern art, even the occasional handshake or cuddle - anything will do, so long as it contributes to the awareness that in worship we are in the presence of the loving, but eternally deep and infinitely wide mystery we call God.

Calvin Coolidge said that it is only when men begin to worship that they begin to grow. As we have discovered, worship is for our benefit rather than God's, but that is not to say that it can be in any sense man-centred; its whole aim must be to make contact with God, and to build up a relationship between him and his people.

In the end, the acid test is whether that relationship becomes real or not. If it does, then that worship, whatever it may look like to the outsider, is right; and if it does not, then however hallowed by history and valued by the traditionalists, it is time that that Church looks for another way of worshipping their God.

We have seen the extraordinary customs used in prayer and praise. To possess a sense *of* the ridiculous is one thing; to find a sense *in* the ridiculous is quite another – particularly a sense of the presence of God.

13 *Come in and Choose your Harp*

My maternal grandmother, just before she died, gazed at a space at the bottom of her bed, and while an expression of great happiness crossed her face, said, 'Frank!' This wasn't me, but her first husband after whom I was named, and he had died thirty years before. She saw, or thought she saw, someone who was much loved, and who had come to welcome her to whatever lay beyond that deathbed. I would regard this story, which my mother told me, as quite eerie, if it were not that so many other people have recounted similar stories of their relatives. A doctor once told me that in his professional opinion this was just a final hallucination of a dying brain – but I've wondered about it ever since.

You can hardly pick up a newspaper or comic book without seeing cartoons of the dead sitting on damp clouds, wearing night-shirts and strumming harps, and the variations of St Peter at the Pearly Gates range from the corny to the hilarious.

The obituary columns of the local papers raise another aspect of death – the pawky and sentimental. The grief and sorrow is all too real, yet the poetry is embarrassing rubbish, and to put it in the paper as a message to the dead is absurd.

But all these things make us think. Is the conviction of a life after this one just a naïve fantasy? Or is the idea that St Peter has a standing order with his local newsagent a silly concept tacked on to something much more real? It is worth looking at, for if there is evidence for life after death, the possibility of it is of crucial importance to us all.

Philosophers have been finding arguments in favour of immortality ever since Plato, but there are three that carry most weight these days.

Firstly, there is the fact of Universal Desire. In all history and every culture, from the Stone Age people who buried their simple grave goods with their dead, to the Pharoahs who build pyramids to house their spirits, every civilization has had its way of expressing its conviction that the dead live on. It is a universal belief that has only in recent centuries been challenged by materialistic philosophies. Belief in life after death is a basic state one has to be educated out of. Left on their own everyone believes in some kind of continuation after death; in fact millions accept an eternity of life who cannot think what to do on a rainy afternoon. It is a universal desire.

As a universal desire it is one of many. We have a desire for food, and though we may be starving, we know that there is such a thing as food to eat. We have a desire for the opposite sex, it is a built-in part of us, and we know that the opposite sex does exist. We have a desire for liberty, and though we may have lived in a totalitarian state all our lives, that yearning will never be quenched until that desire is satisfied. We have a desire for truth, and though we may not be able to take much of it at a time, we know that it exists, and we will not rest until people have told it to us.

There are, in fact, no deep-seated desires in human beings that cannot be satisfied if the circumstances are right, no needs to which there is not an adequate satisfaction – somewhere. We do not have universal desires for things that do not exist.

Then why should our profound need for life after death be different? Why should this be the only desire that has no answer, and cannot be satisfied?

The conclusion we must come to is that if life has any

pattern about it at all, or any symmetry, then there ought to be life after death.

Another argument is based on the Incompleteness of Life. Everything in this world has certain abilities; a bird has wings and flits from bough to bough, a fly can stand upside-down on the ceiling, and a fish can be luminous. The obvious thing is that a fish cannot stand upside-down on the ceiling, a bird cannot light up in the dark, and a fly can't flit (he can buzz, but not flit), and it is interesting to ask why not.

These creatures have abilities that are used to the uttermost, abilities that are designed and controlled to do certain things, and they haven't any abilities to spare. If we tried for months to teach a budgerigar to say

> Shall I compare thee to a summer's day?
> Thou art more lovely and more temperate.

we might be able to manage it with a really bright budgerigar. But to get one to continue the Shakespeare sonnet and 'shake the darling buds of May' would be impossible. For, sad as it may be, budgerigars are not designed to recite Shakespeare. Nowhere in the natural kingdom do we find more abilities than opportunities to use them – except in man. We are the exception.

Here we meet people who have locked up within themselves creative abilities of hand, mind and soul, that are far greater than their opportunities to use them. There are never enough years to fully employ those talents, never enough chances to be as fulfilled as they could be. So often, at funerals, one hears the words, 'What a terrible waste! How much more they could have done had they lived! All those energies and abilities gone!'

Why, when nothing else in this world has its abilities left unused, should mankind be the exception? If the destiny of the animal world is to be fulfilled, then man's destiny must assume a life beyond death in order to complete it.

Turning to a third argument, Life is Unjust.

It is a truism to admit that life is unfair to some people. Everyone knows nice, blameless people who do not cause any trouble, but it seems to follow them around just the same. There are others who break all the rules and yet seem to get away with everything scot free. Usually we do reap what we sow, but there are enough exceptions to make the injustice of this world very disturbing to us.

For we all feel that there *ought* to be justice; not just law and order, but natural justice. On those occasions when the courts do not reflect our feeling for natural justice there is an uproar of indignant letters to the papers and callers to radio phone-in programmes. We, as a community, employ policemen, make laws, appoint judges and magistrates, and keep prisons for those who do wrong. We also, on the plus side, give honours and medals to people who give special service to the community. All this is based on our assumption of natural justice, and we do our best to see that it is observed in our society. There is, underpinning our community life, an assumption that life ought to be just.

But it isn't, not on its own! Which leads to the point that if life is unjust here, there ought to be some continuation of it where justice is completed, goodness rewarded and evil punished. Either we have to admit that our assumption of justice is just pie-in-the-sky, or that there is a life after death.

Moving away from theoretical arguments to practical things – is there any hard evidence for life after death?

There are thousands of stories of ghostly appearances, and dozens of explanations for them. I have personally interviewed many people who have claimed to see and hear ghosts in the places where they saw them, and I must admit that I found them all utterly sincere. But let us for the moment concede that many, if not most, of these apparitions can be put down to fancies and fallacies of one kind or another. A further proportion may be deliberate fraud, and others may be due to natural laws of thought transference of which we know nothing yet. Even if these causes could account for 99.9 per cent, there only has to be *one* genuine ghost, one out of all the world and all history, to prove that death is not the end.

The same principle applies to spiritualism. Even if we uncharitably call the vast proportion of all mediums guilty of fraud, self-delusion, wish-fulfilment, or using purely natural phenomena, there only has to be *one* genuine case of something or someone communicating with us to demonstrate that there is some sort of reality beyond the grave, be it good or bad.

In recent years, because of the astounding advances of modern medicine, people have been brought back from *just over* the brink of death. Many books and articles have been written by people who have experienced the beginnings of what it is like to die, and have been revived to tell us about it. The astounding thing is that they all tell variations of the same story – of looking at themselves from the outside, of hearing what is going on, of beautiful sounds, warm acceptance, and welcoming loved ones. One bishop who had this experience told me that it had completely obliterated any fear of death he might have had, and that he was looking forward to it again. Were this just a case of dying brain cells or a trick of human memory, one would expect that the experiences would be widely varied, depending on the individuals' expectations, and their backgrounds; but no, the story from all is very much the same.

All these arguments are non-religious, and although, neither separately nor added together, do they amount to any kind of proof that death is not the end, they are nevertheless respectable evidence for some kind of immortality.

The Christian, however, does not approach the subject from this angle. It is not immortality that interests him but resurrection; for nowhere in the New Testament is life after death argued – it is *assumed.* In fact Christians feel somewhat out of place with disembodied spirits and 'things that go bump in the night'. Even disembodied *souls* don't count very high, for resurrection means a body, not an ethereal wisp of ectoplasm. If John Brown's body lies a-mouldering in the grave and his soul goes marching on, it can march somewhere else as far as the Christian is concerned, for we are marching to the sound of a distant drum which beats to a different rhythm.

The starting point is that first Resurrection; it was the bomb site for an explosion of God's grace that was at the best startling, and at the worst strange, mysterious, and 'other'. If the paradoxical God we have been thinking about is in charge, we cannot think of an immortality of life continuing as it does now, but of a resurrection that is surprising and startling and very different.

Here we live in time and space, but the spiritual dimension probably has neither. How far the logic and laws of this world are reflected in the next there is no way of knowing. It is bound to be a totally different experience, where the laws of paradox and grace rule supreme. As Peter Pan said, 'Dying must be a very great adventure!' So, even if we knew what lay beyond the grave, we probably wouldn't be able to make sense of it.

But the Christian holds on to the one great certainty that is common to both this life and supernatural life; the love of God as shown in Jesus. He is the only common quality, the safety rope between the two worlds. Greater than our sense of worthlessness, our despair over the problems we leave behind, our sorrow for broken relationships, or our bafflement over whatever lies beyond, is our sense of the love of God. That love, demonstrated in the sacrifice of Jesus, is the only basis for the Christian's hope and understanding of life after death.

If Jesus' picture of God as a loving father is right, then we can safely make some deductions from that. He loves us, and would not let anything happen to us that is not to our ultimate benefit.

What loving father would cause, or even allow, the personality of his child to be abolished? He would encourage the child, teach the child, even punish the child – the one thing he would never do is to kill the child, which is what abolishing the personality amounts to. All that we have found out about God confirms that he loves human beings as people, and that love can only be continued if we continue as people. If our earthly bodies break down or wear out, then in a new life we must have bodies that are suitable there in order that we may remain as recognizable and individual people.

Survival of personality also means, of course, survival of memory, character and relationships, otherwise personality is empty.

God cannot love us as *things* which cannot respond to that love; only as people who can love him back in a rich diversity of expression. This is why the Resurrection is such a crucial thing for the Christian. Jesus survived as a person, changed certainly, but still himself. He said, 'Because I live, you will live also'. Christians believe this, bet their afterlife on the love of God, and take the appearances of the Risen Christ as an example of the spiritual body each will be given in their turn.

Any other evidence for life after death from philosophy or psychic phenomena is interesting but irrelevant, for in thinking of resurrection the Christian has gone beyond them.

To go further than this in thinking about life after death

runs the risk of idle speculation and morbid curiosity. Someone once worked out from the Book of Revelation what the dimensions of the heavenly Jerusalem were, divided into it the statistics of however many people had ever lived, hazarded a guess as to when the world would end, and came up with the answer that we would all have three square feet to stand up in! There have been many similarly useless exercises. One thing only does a Christian need to know – that God is there. Like a dog barking outside a door, he doesn't know what furniture is in that room, and he doesn't care, he knows only that his master is there – that is all that matters to him. All that matters to a Christian is that in any life after death God is there; and this conviction colours his attitude to death and the business of living.

There is a legend that once there was a nobleman who kept a fool. This dwarf, dressed in motley, had to keep the household amused on long winter nights, and was the only one who could be brutally honest with everyone and get away with it. When he was appointed, his master gave him the staff with the pig's bladder on the end with the words, 'Keep it until we find a better fool.'

Years passed, and when the nobleman was on his deathbed he said to the fool,

'I must shortly leave you.'

'And where are you going?' asked the fool.

'Into another world.'

'And when will you come back?'

'Never!'

'Never? And what preparations have you made for your entertainment where you are going?'

'None at all,' said the nobleman.

'None at all?' replied the fool. 'Here, take my staff, for you are a better fool than I am.'

Which brings us to the subject of heaven and hell, the subject of more idle speculation, hell-fire sermons, and ribald humour than anything else connected with religion. Conjured-up pictures of St Peter looking horrified when a coachload from the Mothers Union arrives at the Pearly Gates; Lucifer in despair as he fills warehouse after warehouse with the bodies of left wingers because they're too green to burn, or supplying dentures to those who can't gnash their teeth, amuse everybody - God included, I suspect.

For myself, I reckon that heaven and hell are not places, but a state, a state of being near God; and that this is as close a definition of both heaven and hell as we need.

The reward offered to Christians is an eternity of the knowledge and love of God. The 'pay', if we can call it that, is to be able to love him and serve him better. The 'pay' for loving our neighbour is, because we shall know him and understand him better, being able to love and serve him more.

To anyone who genuinely loves God and his neighbour this is heaven. But to anyone who doesn't, however much they might pretend that they do, it is bound to be sheer hell. It is a bit like the tramp to whom a lady said severely, 'Haven't you ever been offered work?' 'Yes, once,' replied the tramp, 'but apart from that I've been shown nothing but kindness.'

Let us imagine a man who in his youth had the ability and opportunities to take up an interesting and useful career as, say, a doctor, but decided that he could make more money more quickly by running a slot machine arcade. After a few years he finds the job both boring and useless, and by now he realizes that he is on a treadmill going nowhere; the opportunity for any kind of development has gone. This is primarily because he has changed within himself, and can no longer find the single-minded dedication and idealism he would need. He has years of his life before him, but is trapped between pointless triviality and unemployment, with nothing to look forward to but weary self-contempt.

We don't need physical torments, or little devils roasting people over fires, to make a hell; we do quite well constructing our own. We do not need even Bible-sounding phrases like being cast into gross darkness (which as the schoolboy said, is 144 times more murky than ordinary darkness); in reality we draw the curtains ourselves.

The very concept of heaven and hell raises all sorts of questions like, 'How can anyone enjoy heaven as long as there is one person in hell?' At the very least it would be a touch insensitive!

It also begs a far deeper question that has occupied religious minds for centuries. It has seemed to some that God chooses one person and not another; he puts his finger on a man, leaving his neighbour untouched. Why is this? And why do some people respond so readily to him, and others do not?

There is another factor. If God is above time and space and knows what is going to happen to us because he can see the future, then there must be a predictable fatefulness about everything we do. How can this be squared with our individual liberty of mind and conscience – what has happened to our freedom to choose?

This is a subject that has kept theologians arguing ever since Luther and Calvin; but if we look at the dispute sideways we can see two main points that stand out.

The first is that one of the few free choices everyone has in life is to choose or reject Christ. It is a free choice, because no other kind of choice would be acceptable to God; for he wants us to be not unwilling conscripts, but loving followers. God's offer of a new life is open to all. As the hymn puts it:

> He wills that all the fallen race
> Should turn, repent, and live;
> His pardoning grace to all is free.

The second point is that we are dealing here with the real contradiction of human free choice as against God's foreknowledge. Attempts to blend the two ideas have usually ended in unconvincing confusion. Why not admit that it is another of those mysteries to which there can be no logical answer except in the nature of a loving but paradoxical God?

So to sum up: the Christian puts his trust not in general theories of immortality, but in the love of God as shown in the Resurrection of Jesus. If we live with him, and die with him, we shall be raised with him.

I had always been puzzled by the passage in St John's Gospel where Jesus says, 'In my father's house are many mansions.' The whole thing became clear when I discovered that the word really means 'resting-places', and it was another of Jesus' dramatic word pictures.

It was the custom in the East for caravans of travellers to rest every night at a secure and watered camp-site. When they approached one they would send a dragoman ahead to draw some water from the well, light the fire, and then return to guide them to it. In this passage Jesus pictured himself as the dragoman, the trail-blazer on our spiritual journey.

> 'There are many resting-places in my Father's house; otherwise I should have told you. I am going there to prepare a place for you. And if I go and prepare a place for you, I will come back and take you to be with me that you also may be where I am.'

The clear message to Jesus' followers is that as long as we stay with his people and follow his way, he will lead us safely on our journey, even when it crosses the Valley of the Shadow of Death.

14 *Call the Next Witness!*

It would be an amusing thought to imagine Jesus saying to his disciples just before he finally left them, 'Oh, by the way, I've one final instruction. Go out and convert the world for me – there's good chaps!'

At which the disciples would have said, 'Who . . . us?'

But this would not be true to what actually happened. It was obvious from the beginning that the followers were not just listeners but helpers; they were taught about the new Kingdom of God, trained to preach and live it, and sent out in small groups, eventually numbering up to seventy.

The early Christians were fond of calling their religion not Christianity but 'The Way'; it was a pilgrimage to be taken, a journey to tread, and a travelling and preaching ministry.

For to share in Jesus' life means to share in his work of proclaiming his upside-down Kingdom with his inside-out methods; so the message to us is 'Yes – you!'

If Jesus were on trial for being the Son of God, and we were the unwilling but truthful witnesses before the court, when the prosecution called for the next witness, would our evidence be enough to convict him? If not, the look he would give us from the dock would be a very sad one, for Christians are, as part of their faith, called to witness to what they have seen.

At this point most churchgoers curl up and go into their shells, for we live in a country that has been half preached to death, and where people regard talking about their souls as even more indecent than talking about their underwear. Most

Christians do not feel either capable of arguing the toss with an atheist, or knocking on strange doors like a Jehovah's Witness.

This obviously lays on every church the responsibility to train and equip its members; but it also lays on every member the obligation to know as much about their faith as a Communist does about Karl Marx.

The picture has sometimes been drawn of the Church as a kind of spiritual lighthouse, shining its beam far into a dark world. I much prefer the picture of the Church as a lifeboat station, where the coxswain and crew don't sit tight waiting for the shipwrecked to come to them – but go out and get them.

When it comes to the methods and ways of sharing what we believe with others, there are a few tips that can be gleaned from broadcasting techniques. For working in the media are hundreds of Christian professional broadcasters who have spent years preoccupied with the question: 'What makes a good communicator, and in particular, a good *Christian* communicator?'

The first rule is always to be human. The best broadcasters are not afraid to laugh, make mistakes, get angry, get the time wrong, or do any of the normal fallible things that are the marks of being human. When a newsreader said the weather would consist of 'frog and fost', everyone was delighted. When the lady newscaster's earring fell off in the middle of the television news we were secretly pleased. When the protester who dug up the cricket pitch at Headingley appeared on television, the Yorkshire interviewer fizzed with outraged fury at this act of sacrilege, and we all sympathized. When the very new female presenter announced, 'It is twelve o'clock Greenwich . . . meantime here is the news,' we all said understandingly, 'Ah well, she'll learn!' It is all so natural, so like us, so human.

As long as it doesn't cross the border into incompetence, most broadcasters are pleased when some signs of real humanity unwittingly occur. Although what we see on television and hear on radio is the end result of a long line of technological miracles, it only succeeds as communication if those dots on a cathode ray tube, or vibrations of a loudspeaker cone, can convey humanity – real people.

We all recognize the times when, in a rather predictable programme, the unexpected happens, the people react naturally, and the programme suddenly starts to live. Humanity communicates; inhumanity doesn't.

One of the most disliked modern inventions is the telephone answering machine, doubtless to be followed soon by talking computers in the home. Like most people I loathe having to use them, useful though they may be, because I do not want to talk to a machine. Communication is one aspect of what being human means, and communication can only happen between human beings. All machines can do is to record, store or transmit our humanity; and they are judged by how faithfully they can do it.

Jesus was not afraid to show his humanity, for in the Gospels we see him weeping, hungry, tired, caring, angry, and vulnerable. It was his authority that made him respected; it was his humanity that made him loved.

So when the right time and opportunity comes for a Christian to share his or her faith, the accent must be on our humanity. Christians are not perfect, and our lives are not perfect, for doubts and difficulties come to Christians and non-Christians alike. To try to pretend that we are above such trivial worldly problems will get us nowhere. If we are hurt by life we should not be ashamed to show it.

It is, to say the least, unconvincing to be like the hero of the Western film who came home to find his ranch burned to the ground, his family kidnapped, and his best cowboy dead among the smoking ruins, and who, strapping on his gun said, 'I'll get them dirty rats, but first, folks, I'll sing you a little song.' God will help us to overcome the trouble, but not to give the false impression that it hasn't happened, or that it hasn't hurt.

We must also be prepared to laugh at life and at ourselves. Clive James once wrote, 'A sense of humour is common-sense dancing – never trust anyone without a sense of humour, because they have no judgement.' Only a truly religious person can laugh at religion and God. To see the funny side and the absurdities of ourselves and the Church is a sign of grace and real humanity.

We should also enjoy life. Just as a father enjoys seeing his children revelling in the sunshine of a summer afternoon on the back lawn, and in the paddling pool, so God enjoys seeing us picking a few daisies on our way. The Puritans stimulated an unknown poet to write:

> The puritan through life's garden goes,
> Picks the thorn and casts away the rose,
> And thinks by this peculiar whim
> To please the God who gave it him.

As G. K. Chesterton said, 'religion is far too serious to be solemn about it.' It is no credit to God if we spurn the humanity he has given us, and don't enjoy the world he has put us in.

Christians ought, in all honesty, to admit their own ignorance. Some mistakenly think that their witness to their faith is helped by having snap answers to every problem in the world. This is not only untrue, but demonstrates a small mind and a lack of sympathy for others. In fact, the Christian may well have *more* problems than others, because he has to grapple with the difficulties of living his faith in an uncaring world.

Throughout the previous chapters I have been very conscious of having to say so often, 'We don't know', or 'This is a mystery beyond the human mind.' It may be unsatisfactory and untidy to leave loose ends all over the world, but we have no need to apologize for it. Christians carry far more conviction if they are honest and say they don't know, than if they hang on to any answer for the sake of it. For ignorance is a sign of humanity, and the willingness to admit it a sign of integrity. A know-all is always unattractive; a religious know-all is both unattractive and unbelievable.

Christians are not necessarily any better or wiser than anyone else, and are as vulnerable to the stresses and vagaries of life as anyone else. The difference is that we have found one truth that changes and helps us, the love of God shown in Jesus. We are not arrogantly looking for people who are enjoying themselves so that we can tell them to stop it, but simply one lot of starving people telling another lot where to find the food aid.

If being human is one factor in communicating, respecting the person we are talking to is another. It means respecting them, respecting their views, and respecting their feelings.

No broadcaster stands a chance of communicating with his listeners if he doesn't start where they are. He cannot afford to over- or under-estimate their intelligence. A well-known lady broadcaster once completely damned a radio station by saying that it was staffed by 'lascivious milkmen' – and we know the low-level mindless bonhomie that implies. No one likes to be talked-down to, least of all by their own radio set; so we switch off.

No one likes, either, to be 'got at', bullied, or pressurized; and broadcasters know that attractive persuasion is the best way to achieve results. People are much more likely to say Yes if they have every opportunity to say No. In religious areas attempts to pressure people are always counter-productive, and in any case wrong; for if God gives people the chance to say No, then so must we. Donald Soper once said, 'You can always tell the people who have been done good to, by the hunted look on their faces.' It is not a look of which God approves.

Jesus respected the people he talked to by starting where they were, and adjusting what he said to suit their circumstances. When he was with farmers he talked about crops, when he was with shepherds, about sheep; he talked about their needs and their cares, using the fabric of their lives to spin the stories. He cared for them and respected them, and they knew it.

The people we meet are not just numbers in a heavenly computer, or statistics in a church roll, but real people whom God created and for whom Christ died – he loves them, and so must we. Anything we say to them, and even more, the time we give listening to them, must be because we care about them as people, and that care must show.

So when the time is right, and the opportunity is right, we may be asked to share with them what we know about God. We must do it gently and sensitively. A musician once said, 'If I wanted to sell you a Stradivarius violin, I wouldn't do it by hitting you over the head with it, but by playing the nicest tune I could on it.'

To change the metaphor, imagine showing a child a bird's nest in a hedge. We wouldn't slam the five-bar gate, saw down half the bush and shout, 'There it is!' But we would tiptoe quietly up to it, part the branches slowly, and whisper.

So must our attitude be to sharing our insights into God with others; it must be done with a quiet sensitivity for our listeners' opinions, and a respect for their feelings.

A third element is to gain the respect of our listener. This is the hardest part; it often takes a long time, and is sometimes impossible.

A few people in broadcasting manage this instantaneously by their transparent honesty, integrity and character; some others do it with a bubbling and attractive enthusiasm. But for most broadcasters it is a long haul, a gradually developing relationship until the listener gets to the point of trusting his abilities, and approving of his reactions.

Jesus was not only respected by a great number of people who heard him and met him; but even more, he was loved. The things he said and did were valued and remembered, because of the impression he made, and the kind of person he was.

So in our conversations with neighbours over the fence, or with work-mates in the canteen, the credibility of what we say is based on what we are like in ourselves, and whether we have gained any respect in their eyes. Only when they have come to respect us as people will they come to respect anything we say.

These then are three signs of good broadcasters: to be human, to respect the listener, and be respected by them. Put them together and you have a formidable communicator indeed.

These same three factors are important for the Christian witness too; but I would hesitate to put them forward as any kind of technique. Like most people, I am highly suspicious of experts in the art of communication who write turgid papers like one I received called 'Towards an Anthropological Philosophy of Communication', which proved to be totally unreadable.

To be human, to respect others, and to be respected by them, are signs of people who communicate well, because they are like that. A loving, caring Christian heart does all of these things as naturally and instinctively as Jesus did. The secrets of communication, such as they are, cannot be 'mugged-up' from the text books of an American business school, but are slowly grown in the depths of human character.

Perhaps, when you boil it all down, failures in communication are really failures of love. The loving, outgoing Christian heart knows not only what to say, but when and how to say it.

Biblical References

CHAPTER 1 *Unscrewing the Inscrutable*

'. . . the hairs of your head are numbered', Matthew 10.30

'. . . revealed them to little children', Matthew 11.25

Faith . . . biased in favour of the childlike, Matthew 18.1–4

CHAPTER 2 *Non-existent – but Easy*

'Help me to overcome my unbelief', Mark 9.24

CHAPTER 3 *Dog Spelled Backwards*

'God is Love', 1 John 4.8

. . . driven by starvation into Egypt, The full story of the journey of the Israelites into Egypt and their subsequent enslavement is told from Genesis chapter 46 to the early chapters of Exodus.

God speaking to Moses, Exodus 3.14 and 6.2

Yahweh speaks in thunder and lightning, Exodus 19.16–25

. . . guides his people with smoke and fire, Exodus 13.20–2

'. . . from whence cometh my help', Psalm 121.1

'a father wouldn't do this to his children . . .', Matthew 7.11

'Now we see a poor reflection . . .', 1 Corinthians 13.12

CHAPTER 4 *God's Fingerprints*

The story of Elijah is told in 1 Kings chapter 17 to 2 Kings chapter 2.

'You are Elijah!', Matthew 16.13 and Mark 8.28

'. . . reflection in a mirror', 1 Corinthians 13.12

CHAPTER 5 *Strewth!*

'What is truth?', John 18.38

'I am the truth', John 14.6
'. . . keeping truth for ever', Psalm 46.6
Prodigal Son, Luke 15.11–32
Good Samaritan, Luke 10.25–37
Lord's Prayer, Matthew 6.9–15 and Luke 11.1–4

CHAPTER 6 *The Inside-out Teacher*

His home town of Nazareth, Mark 6.1–6 and Luke 4.16–30
Mary Magdalene, John 20.16
Storm on the lake, Mark 4.35–9
Women provided for Jesus, Luke 8.2–3
'The people were astonished', Luke 4.32 and Mark 1.22
'By what authority? . . .' Luke 20.2
'Happy are those . . .', Matthew 5.3–12 and Luke 6.20–3
Love your enemies, Matthew 5.43–4
The rich ruler, Mark 10.17–22
Unexpected guests, Luke 11.5–8
Lost piece of silver, Luke 15.8–10
Our daily bread, Matthew 6.11
Ship's cable . . . eye of a needle, Mark 10.25
No longer strangers, Ephesians 2.19
'Don't . . . be called "Master"', Matthew 23.10.
Put the service of God first, Matthew 6.33
Build on the rock, Matthew 7.24–7
Disappeared into the wilderness, Matthew 4.1–11 and Luke 4.1–13

CHAPTER 7 *The Upside-down Revolutionary*

The Song of Mary, Luke 2.46–55
The Good Samaritan, Luke 10.25–37
'The Law of God', Deuteronomy 6.5 and Leviticus 19.18
Levites helped Aaron, Numbers 3.5–10
Assyria . . . transported the ten tribes of Israel, 2 Kings chapter 17
'The first shall be last . . .', Matthew 20.16 and Luke 14.7–11
Beatitudes, Matthew 5.3–12

CHAPTER 8 *A Picture Book Saviour*

Adam, Eve and the snake, Genesis chapter 3
Towers without an estimate, Luke 14.28–30
Houses on good and bad foundations, Matthew 7.24–9
Starting a new vineyard, Matthew 21.33
'on this rock . . .', Matthew 16.18
'Are you also from Galilee?', John 7.52
Simon Peter at Jesus' trial, Matthew 26.73
St Paul . . . Isaiah, Romans 4.25; 5.6–8; Galatians 1.4; and Isaiah 53.5
'. . . a ransom for many', Mark 10.45
Jesus as sacrificial lamb, John 1.29 and 1 Peter 1.19
'Christ came as High Priest . . .', Hebrews 9.11
'This is my body . . .', Luke 22.19–20

CHAPTER 9 *The Back-to-Front Surprise*

The Gospel accounts of the Resurrection are found in Matthew chapter 28, Mark chapter 16, Luke chapter 24 and John chapters 20–1
Second appearance . . ., John 20.26–9
Coming of the Holy Spirit, Acts chapter 2
Joseph of Arimathea, Mark 15.42–7
Matthew, the tax-gatherer, Matthew 9.9; 10.3
St Paul's conversion experience, Acts 9.1–22 and 1 Corinthians 15.8
'If Christ has not been raised . . .', 1 Corinthians 15.14
St John . . . confesses his ignorance . . ., 1 John 3.2
'. . . goats . . . sheep', Matthew 25.31–46
Grain of wheat, 1 Corinthians 15.35–44
. . . thought they were drunk, Acts 2.6–13

CHAPTER 10 *The Offensive Weapon*

The armour of God, Ephesians 6.10–20
The first Whitsunday, Acts chapter 2
'comforter . . . spirit of truth', John 14.26; 15.26

'It seemed good to the Holy Spirit and to us', Acts 15.28
Philip . . . by the main road, Acts 8.26–40
Peter . . . Roman centurion, Acts chapter 10
Christian in Damascus, Acts 9.10–18
Gifts of the Holy Spirit, 1 Corinthians chapter 13
Fruits of the Spirit, Galatians 5.22–3
Individual gifts, 1 Corinthians chapter 12

CHAPTER 11 *The Church Idiotic*

Christ's appearance to Paul, Acts 9.1–22
Peter's statement, Mark 8.29
The Last Supper, Matthew 26.26–9; Mark 14.22–5; Luke 22.19–20 and 1 Corinthians 11.23–6
When two or three . . . are gathered, Matthew 18.20
Church as Temple of God, 1 Peter 2.5
. . . as wife of Christ, Ephesians 5.23
. . . as bride of Christ, 2 Corinthians 11.2
. . . as body of Christ, Ephesians 4.15–16

CHAPTER 12 *A Sense of the Ridiculous*

. . . a clip round the ear . . ., Luke 11.11–13
. . . borrow some bread . . ., Luke 11.5–8
Bent magistrate, Luke 18.2–8
Jacob's Ladder, Genesis 28.10–22
'Stewards of the mysteries of God', 1 Corinthians 4.1

CHAPTER 13 *Come in and Choose your Harp*

'Because I live . . .', John 14.19
Many mansions, John 14.2–3

CHAPTER 14 *Call the Next Witness!*

Small groups . . . seventy, Mark 6.7–13 and Luke 10.1–17
Jesus . . . vulnerable, John 11.35; Mark 4.2; John 4.6; and John 19.28

MORE BOOKS FROM

DAVID ADAM

The Edge of Glory

Modern prayers in the Celtic tradition by the vicar of a country parish in North Yorkshire. With line illustrations.

ERIC LIDDELL

The Disciplines of the Christian Life

The first British publication of this newly discovered work by the hero of *Chariots of Fire.* A practical guide to Christian living.

KITTY MUGGERIDGE

Gazing on Truth

Meditations on reality, opening eyes to a wider view of what is real.

'Her text is studded with lovely quotations . . . it is a wide ranging set of truths'.
The Bookseller

PETER MULLEN

Rural Rites

Tales from the fictional Yorkshire village of Marton-on-t'Moor, seen through the eyes of its much-harassed vicar.

'We will accept that the characters do not legally exist but, my goodness, they are all recognizable . . .'
Lincolnshire Standard

Country Matters

A further look at the high spirited antics of life at Marton.

'. . . may earn him the title "the James Herriot of the Church of England".'
Radio Oxford

MARGARET CUNDIFF

Called to be Me

Lively reminiscences of a deaconess in a Yorkshire parish. With line illustrations.

'Realistic and hilarious.'
Christian Bookseller

Following on

Another enjoyable invitation to meet the people who share in the life of this busy woman minister.
With line illustrations.

I'd Like You to Meet . . .

And wherever she meets them – broadcasting studio, supermarket, London bus or in her parish – all have enriched her life. Here she passes that richness on.

'Margaret Cundiff is communicating God's love and joyousness all the time.'
C of E Newspaper

BRENDA COURTIE

Not Quite Heaven

A heart-warming account by a Liverpool housewife of deepening Christian experience through everyday life.

'A book to make you laugh, cry and sing.'
Christian Herald